10

SOCCER PRACTICE GAMES

Third Edition

JOSEPH A. LUXBACHER, PhD

Human Kinetics

Library of Congress Cataloging-in-Publication Data

Luxbacher, Joe.
  Soccer practice games / Joseph A. Luxbacher. -- 3rd ed.
    p. cm.
  ISBN-13: 978-0-7360-8366-9 (soft cover)
  ISBN-10: 0-7360-8366-9 (soft cover)
  1. Soccer--Training. 2. Soccer--Coaching. I. Title.
  GV943.9.T7L895 2010
  796.334--dc22

                              2010002229

ISBN-10: 0-7360-8366-9 (print)
ISBN-13: 978-0-7360-8366-9 (print)

Copyright © 2010, 2003, 1995 by Joseph A. Luxbacher

Acquisitions Editor: Tom Heine; **Developmental Editor:** Carla Zych; **Assistant Editors:** Michael Bishop and Martha Gullo; **Copyeditor:** Mary Rivers; **Graphic Designer:** Joe Buck; **Graphic Artist:** Tara Welsch; **Cover Designer:** Keith Blomberg; **Photographer (cover):** © Human Kinetics; **Photographer (interior):** Neil Bernstein except as otherwise noted; photos on pages 1, 31, 79, 119, and 175 © Human Kinetics; photos on pages 5, 55, 103, and 149 © Amy Myers/Fotolia; **Photo Asset Manager:** Laura Fitch; **Visual Production Assistant:** Joyce Brumfield; **Photo Production Manager:** Jason Allen; **Art Manager:** Kelly Hendren; **Associate Art Manager:** Alan L. Wilborn; **Printer:** United Graphics

We thank University of Pittsburgh in Pittsburgh, Pennsylvania, for assistance in providing the location for the photo shoot for this book.

Human Kinetics books are available at special discounts for bulk purchase. Special editions or book excerpts can also be created to specification. For details, contact the Special Sales Manager at Human Kinetics.

Printed in the United States of America   10 9 8 7 6 5 4 3

The paper in this book is certified under a sustainable forestry program.

Human Kinetics
Web site: www.HumanKinetics.com

United States: Human Kinetics
P.O. Box 5076
Champaign, IL 61825-5076
800-747-4457
e-mail: humank@hkusa.com

Canada: Human Kinetics
475 Devonshire Road Unit 100
Windsor, ON N8Y 2L5
800-465-7301 (in Canada only)
e-mail: info@hkcanada.com

Europe: Human Kinetics
107 Bradford Road
Stanningley
Leeds LS28 6AT, United Kingdom
+44 (0) 113 255 5665
e-mail: hk@hkeurope.com

Australia: Human Kinetics
57A Price Avenue
Lower Mitcham, South Australia 5062
08 8372 0999
e-mail: info@hkaustralia.com

New Zealand: Human Kinetics
P.O. Box 80
Torrens Park, South Australia 5062
0800 222 062
e-mail: info@hknewzealand.com

E4844

To my dad and mom, Francis and Mary Ann Luxbacher, the finest parents a boy could ever hope for, who always encouraged me to pursue my passions. Their presence will always be with me. And to my children, Eliza and Travis, in hopes that they will also follow their passions and experience as much enjoyment and excitement from their chosen careers as I have with mine.

Contents

1 **Planning Practice Sessions** 1

2 **Warm-Up and Conditioning Games** 5

3 **Dribbling, Shielding, and Tackling Games** 31

4 **Passing and Receiving Games** 55

Game Finder

Game number	Game title	Difficulty rating	Number of players*	Dribbling & shielding	Tackling	Passing & receiving	Shooting	Heading	Goalkeeping	Page number
Chapter 2 Warm-Up and Conditioning Games										
1	Chain Gang	⚽	any							7
2	Hounds and Hares	⚽	(4s)							8
3	Pass and Follow	⚽	5			✓				9
4	Doctor, Doctor	⚽	15+	✓						10
5	Flag Tag	⚽	any	✓						11
6	Dribble Relay	⚽	(4s-6s)	✓						12
7	Twin Tag	⚽	any							13
8	Dribble the Gauntlet	⚽	any	✓		✓				14
9	Dribble Freeze Tag	⚽	any	✓						15
10	Shark Attack	⚽	any	✓						16
11	Team Tag	⚽	12-16	✓						17
12	Toss to Target	⚽⚽	12-20							18
13	Nutmeg Competition	⚽⚽	any	✓		✓				19
14	Pinball Possession	⚽⚽	5-8			✓				20
15	Attack of the Crab Monsters	⚽⚽	11-20	✓						21
16	Sharks and Minnows	⚽⚽	any	✓	✓					22
17	Join the Hunt	⚽⚽	12-20	✓		✓				23
18	Team Handball	⚽⚽	12-20							24
19	Takeover Competition	⚽⚽	any	✓						25
20	Pass Though the Moving Goal	⚽⚽	any	✓		✓				26
21	Target Practice	⚽⚽	6			✓				27
22	Running the Bases	⚽⚽	16-20	✓						28
23	Chase the Coyote	⚽⚽⚽	any	✓		✓				29
24	Shooting Fish in a Barrel	⚽⚽⚽	any	✓		✓				30

*Parentheses indicate that players are divided into groups of the number indicated.

⚽ Beginner   ⚽⚽ Intermediate   ⚽⚽⚽ Advanced

Game number	Game title	Difficulty rating	Number of players	Dribbling & shielding	Tackling	Passing & receiving	Shooting	Heading	Goalkeeping	Page number
Chapter 3 Dribbling, Shielding, and Tackling Games										
25	Shadow the Dribbler	⚽	any	✓						33
26	Dribble to Retain Possession	⚽	any	✓						34
27	Release the Hounds	⚽	any	✓						35
28	Magnets	⚽	any	✓						36
29	Red Light, Yellow Light, Green Light	⚽	any	✓						37
30	Starts, Stops, and Turns	⚽	any	✓						38
31	Dribble the Open Goal	⚽	8-16	✓						39
32	Shifting Gears	⚽	any	✓						40
33	Protect Your Ball	⚽⚽	any	✓	✓					41
34	Alleviate Pressure	⚽⚽	any	✓						42
35	Soccer Marbles	⚽⚽	(3s)	✓		✓				43
36	First to the Cone	⚽⚽	any	✓						44
37	Speed Dribble Race	⚽⚽	any	✓						45
38	Slalom Dribbling Relay	⚽⚽	(3s-5s)	✓						46
39	Wolves and Sheep	⚽⚽	any	✓						47
40	Tackle All Balls	⚽⚽	any	✓	✓					48
41	Too Few Balls	⚽⚽	20-24	✓	✓					49
42	Knockout	⚽⚽	10-20	✓	✓					50
43	First to the End Line	⚽⚽	10-20	✓	✓					51
44	Rob the Bank	⚽⚽	any	✓	✓					52
45	Breakout	⚽⚽	any	✓	✓					53
46	Navigate the Channel	⚽⚽⚽	any	✓	✓					54

 Beginner    Intermediate    Advanced

Game number	Game title	Difficulty rating	Number of players	Dribbling & shielding	Tackling	Passing & receiving	Shooting	Heading	Goalkeeping	Page number
Chapter 4 Passing and Receiving Games										
47	Pass Through the Channels	🖤	any	✓		✓				57
48	Connect the Dots	🖤	(5s-8s)	✓		✓				58
49	Around the Square	🖤🖤	12-16			✓				59
50	Find the Open Player	🖤🖤	(4s)			✓				60
51	Tempo Passing	🖤🖤	(4s-5s)			✓				61
52	Bump, Spin, and Do It Again	🖤🖤	(4s)			✓				62
53	Flighted Balls	🖤🖤	10			✓				63
54	Group Ball Juggle	🖤🖤	(3s)			✓				64
55	Toss, Cushion, and Catch	🖤🖤	10-14			✓				65
56	Soccer Dodge Ball	🖤🖤	12-20	✓		✓				66
57	Find Open Space	🖤🖤	(4s)			✓				67
58	Hunt the Fox	🖤🖤	any	✓		✓				68
59	Perimeter Passing	🖤🖤	9 or 12			✓				69
60	Moving Targets	🖤🖤🖤	12-20	✓		✓				70
61	4v4v4	🖤🖤🖤	12			✓				71
62	Large-Group Possession	🖤🖤🖤	15-21			✓				72
63	8v8 (+2) Across the Midline	🖤🖤🖤	18			✓				73
64	Pass to the End Zones	🖤🖤🖤	8-12	✓	✓	✓				74
65	Score Through Multiple Goals	🖤🖤🖤	10-14	✓	✓	✓				75
66	6v3 End to End	🖤🖤🖤	20	✓	✓	✓	✓		✓	76
67	Soccer Volleyball	🖤🖤🖤	10-20			✓		✓		77
68	5 (+5)v5 (+5)	🖤🖤🖤	20-24		✓	✓				78
Chapter 5 Shooting and Finishing Games										
69	Dribble the Maze and Score	🖤	4-6	✓			✓		✓	81
70	Shooting off the Dribble	🖤	8-10	✓			✓		✓	82
71	The Golden Boot	🖤	3	✓			✓		✓	83
72	World Cup Scoring Frenzy	🖤🖤	9-13	✓	✓	✓	✓		✓	84
73	Pressure Finishing	🖤🖤	(4s)				✓		✓	85

 Beginner Intermediate 🖤🖤🖤 Advanced

Game number	Game title	Difficulty rating	Number of players	Dribbling & shielding	Tackling	Passing & receiving	Shooting	Heading	Goalkeeping	Page number
	Chapter 5 Shooting and Finishing Games *(continued)*									
74	Serve and Shoot	●●	7				✓			86
75	3 (+1)v3 (+1) Long-Distance Shooting	●●	10	✓	✓	✓	✓			87
76	Score Through the Central Goal	●●	7-11	✓	✓	✓	✓			88
77	Finishing Crosses	●●	6			✓	✓			89
78	Score off the Breakaway	●●	any	✓			✓			90
79	Toss and Volley to Score	●●	3				✓			91
80	Empty Net	●●	10-14				✓			92
81	3v1 in the Box	●●	6			✓	✓			93
82	Scoring From Set Pieces	●●	8				✓			94
83	Goal-to-Goal Scoring	●●	14	✓		✓	✓			95
84	2v2 to Goal	●●●	11	✓	✓	✓	✓			96
85	Score From Distance	●●●	12	✓	✓	✓	✓			97
86	Shoot to Score	●●●	4	✓	✓		✓			98
87	Numbers-Up Scoring	●●●	12	✓	✓	✓	✓			99
88	Volley Shooting	●●●	8-12				✓			100
89	3v2 to 2v1 Transition Scoring	●●●	14	✓	✓	✓	✓			101
90	Attacking Numbers-Down	●●●	8	✓	✓	✓	✓			102
	Chapter 6 Heading Games									
91	Toss and Head to Score	●	(3s)					✓		105
92	Jack in the Box	●●	(3s)					✓		106
93	Heading Goal to Goal	●●	any					✓		107
94	Heading Race Front to Back	●●	(4s-6s)					✓		108
95	Group Head Juggle	●●	(4s)					✓		109
96	Score off a Flighted Ball	●●	9			✓		✓		110
97	Defensive Heading	●●	(3s)					✓		111
98	Team Heading Competition	●●	any					✓		112
99	Diving Headers	●●●	9-13					✓	✓	113

● Beginner   ●● Intermediate   ●●● Advanced

Game number	Game title	Difficulty rating	Number of players	Dribbling & shielding	Tackling	Passing & receiving	Shooting	Heading	Goalkeeping	Page number
	Chapter 6 Heading Games *(continued)*									
100	1v1 Head to Score	Advanced	6			✓		✓		114
101	3v2 (+ Servers) in the Penalty Area	Advanced	8			✓		✓	✓	115
102	Diving Headers on Multiple Goals	Advanced	10-12					✓		116
103	Toss, Catch, and Head to Score	Advanced	12-16					✓		117
104	5v2 to 5v2 Score by Headers Only	Advanced	10			✓		✓		118
	Chapter 7 Individual and Small-Group Tactical Games									
105	1v1 to Common Goal	Beginner	any	✓	✓					121
106	Defend the End Line (1v1)	Beginner	any	✓	✓					122
107	1v1 to Minigoals	Beginner	4	✓	✓					123
108	Simultaneous 1v1 (+Support)	Intermediate	8	✓	✓					124
109	Attack the Goal Least Defended	Intermediate	6-8	✓	✓	✓				125
110	Attack 1v2	Intermediate	7	✓	✓					126
111	Numbers Down in the Box	Intermediate	5	✓	✓		✓		✓	127
112	Play the Wall (2v1)	Intermediate	(3s)	✓	✓	✓				128
113	Attack the End Line 2v1	Intermediate	3	✓	✓	✓				129
114	2v1 (+1) Transition	Intermediate	4	✓	✓	✓	✓			130
115	Triangular Support (3v1)	Intermediate	(4s)	✓	✓	✓				131
116	Last Player in Defends	Intermediate	5	✓	✓	✓				132
117	2v2 With Support	Intermediate	8	✓	✓	✓				133
118	2v2 (+Targets)	Intermediate	6	✓	✓	✓				134
119	3v2 (+1) Transition	Intermediate	6	✓	✓	✓	✓			135
120	Split the Defense	Intermediate	6	✓	✓	✓				136
121	Possess to Penetrate	Intermediate	8	✓	✓	✓				137
122	Deny Penetration	Intermediate	6	✓	✓	✓				138
123	4v2 (+2) to Four Goals	Intermediate	8	✓	✓	✓	✓		✓	139

Beginner   Intermediate   Advanced

Game number	Game title	Difficulty rating	Number of players	Dribbling & shielding	Tackling	Passing & receiving	Shooting	Heading	Goalkeeping	Page number
Chapter 7 Individual and Small-Group Tactical Games *(continued)*										
124	3v3 (+1) Possession	⚽⚽	7	✓	✓	✓				140
125	Quick Counterattack	⚽⚽	8	✓	✓	✓	✓			141
126	Two-Sided Goals	⚽⚽⚽	10	✓	✓	✓	✓			142
127	Score to Stay	⚽⚽⚽	10	✓	✓	✓	✓		✓	143
128	Three Zone	⚽⚽⚽	12	✓	✓	✓	✓		✓	144
129	Zonal Defending	⚽⚽⚽	8	✓	✓	✓	✓			145
130	Flank Attack	⚽⚽⚽	12	✓	✓	✓	✓	✓	✓	146
131	5v5 (+2) on Six Goals	⚽⚽⚽	12	✓	✓	✓				147
Chapter 8 Large-Group and Team Tactical Games										
132	6v4 (+4) Possession	⚽⚽	14	✓	✓	✓				151
133	Team Attack and Defense (7v5)	⚽⚽	13	✓	✓	✓	✓	✓	✓	152
134	Dribble the End Line to Score	⚽⚽⚽	12-16	✓	✓	✓				153
135	Tactical Dribbling	⚽⚽⚽	12-16	✓	✓	✓	✓	✓	✓	154
136	Four-Goal Contest	⚽⚽⚽	22	✓	✓	✓	✓	✓	✓	155
137	Defend the Counter	⚽⚽⚽	19	✓	✓	✓	✓	✓	✓	156
138	6v6 (+6) to Goal	⚽⚽⚽	20	✓	✓	✓	✓	✓	✓	157
139	Attack With Numbers	⚽⚽⚽	18	✓	✓	✓	✓	✓	✓	158
140	Stretching the Field	⚽⚽⚽	20	✓	✓	✓	✓	✓	✓	159
141	10v5 (+5)	⚽⚽⚽	20	✓	✓	✓		✓	✓	160
142	4v4 Transition to End Zones	⚽⚽⚽	16	✓	✓	✓				161
143	10v5 Breakout	⚽⚽⚽	15	✓	✓	✓				162
144	4v6 Transition to 6v4	⚽⚽⚽	22	✓	✓	✓	✓	✓	✓	163
145	9v9 on Six Minigoals	⚽⚽⚽	18	✓	✓	✓	✓	✓		164
146	4 (+4)v4 (+4) to Full Goals	⚽⚽⚽	18	✓	✓	✓	✓	✓	✓	165
147	Long Service	⚽⚽⚽	20	✓	✓	✓	✓	✓	✓	166
148	Play to Targets	⚽⚽⚽	20	✓	✓	✓	✓	✓		167
149	Hold the Lead	⚽⚽⚽	20	✓	✓	✓	✓	✓	✓	168

 Beginner  Intermediate  Advanced

Game number	Game title	Difficulty rating	Number of players	Dribbling & shielding	Tackling	Passing & receiving	Shooting	Heading	Goalkeeping	Page number
Chapter 8 Large-Group and Team Tactical Games *(continued)*										
150	6v4 Finishing	●●●	22	✓	✓	✓	✓	✓	✓	169
151	Scoring From Distance	●●●	16	✓	✓	✓	✓	✓	✓	170
152	Three-Sided Goals	●●●	20	✓	✓	✓	✓			171
153	Compact the Field	●●●	18	✓	✓	✓	✓			172
154	Pressing to the Attack	●●●	18	✓	✓	✓	✓	✓	✓	173
Chapter 9 Goalkeeping Games										
155	Toss and Catch	●	any						✓	177
156	Saving Skippers	●●	any						✓	178
157	Catching Pingers	●●	any						✓	179
158	Handing Low Balls	●●	10	✓			✓		✓	180
159	Set and Save	●●	2				✓		✓	181
160	Reaction Saves	●●	4				✓		✓	182
161	Rapid-Fire Shoot and Save	●●	6				✓		✓	183
162	Play the Angle	●●	6	✓			✓		✓	184
163	Distribute by Throwing	●●	6			✓			✓	185
164	Distribution Circuit	●●	4						✓	186
165	Control the Goal Box	●●●	16	✓		✓	✓	✓	✓	187
166	Goalie Wars	●●●	any				✓		✓	188
167	Dive to Save (5v2 + 2v5)	●●●	16	✓	✓	✓	✓	✓	✓	189
168	Defend the Two-Sided Goal	●●●	10	✓	✓	✓	✓		✓	190
169	High-Ball Repetition Training	●●●	7			✓		✓	✓	191
170	Aerial Wars	●●●	18			✓	✓	✓	✓	192
171	Save the Breakaway	●●●	any	✓			✓		✓	193
172	Score on Breakaways Only	●●●	7	✓	✓	✓	✓		✓	194
173	Shooter Versus Goalkeeper	●●●	12-16	✓			✓		✓	195
174	Four-Sided Goal	●●●	10	✓	✓	✓	✓		✓	196
175	Organizing the Back Line	●●●	14	✓	✓	✓	✓		✓	197

● Beginner   ●● Intermediate   ●●● Advanced

Foreword

Soccer Practice Games is a "must have" for youth soccer coaches and parents everywhere. Creating an environment for young players that is conducive to learning and having fun is crucial to their technical and tactical development and to their success playing the game. Coach Joe Luxbacher shows you how it's done.

This book is organized in a very easy-to-follow format. Coach Luxbacher provides essential information on planning effective practice sessions and follows it with age appropriate gamelike activities that facilitate the physical, technical, and tactical development of young players. The games are clearly described and accompanied by illustrations and photos to help you select those that will benefit your players the most.

Soccer Practice Games emphasizes the games approach to training youth soccer players. Soccer is a free flowing game with no consistent down time (no time outs); it requires players to make many decisions in a short time span—and to make them on the fly. Therefore the best way for players to master the game is to be immersed in activities that replicate the game. In other words...*young players get better at playing soccer by playing soccer!*

The use of regimented drills that force players into lines to perform choreographed movements slows the pace of player development. And it's a lot less fun!

As the former US Youth Soccer National Director of Coaching Education, I completely support and endorse the games approach to training. As the current Director of Training and Evaluation for Massachusetts Youth Soccer, I implement training programs with games like these on a daily basis. I recommend *Soccer Practice Games* to anyone who coaches youth soccer or who has a child that plays soccer.

Congratulations to Coach Joe Luxbacher on the creation of a great coaching aid!

Tom Goodman, M.Ed.
Director of Training and Evaluation
Massachusetts Youth Soccer

Preface

Soccer! The game evokes an outpouring of passion and emotion rarely equaled within the realm of competitive sport. Known internationally as football, soccer provides a common language for peoples of diverse backgrounds and heritages, creating a bond that transcends political, ethnic, religious, and economic barriers. The national game of nearly every country in Asia, Africa, Europe, and South America, soccer is played daily by more than one billion men, women, and children. More than 150 million registered athletes, including more than 10 million women, play the sport on an official basis. Countless more kick the ball around on an unofficial basis, on sandlots, in playgrounds, and on the back streets of small towns and large cities. These impressive participant numbers are dwarfed by the number of avid fans worldwide who follow the sport on television. In 2006, the average viewership for each match of the month-long (64 matches) World Cup was 93 million. More than three times that number tuned in for the final between Italy and France. To illustrate the magnitude of soccer's following, an estimated 97.5 million people watched the 2008 NFL Super Bowl, generally considered to be America's biggest game.

Soccer's universal appeal does not rest on it being an easy game to play. In fact, soccer may demand more of athletes than any other sport. The game is played on a larger field than any sport except polo (where horses do the bulk of the work!). Players must perform a variety of foot skills under the match pressures of restricted space, limited time, physical fatigue, and determined opponents challenging for the ball. There are no official time-outs during a typical 90-minute match, and substitution is limited. Knowledge of tactics and strategies is essential for successful performance. Decision-making skills are constantly tested as players must respond instantly to changing situations during play. With the exception of the goalkeeper, there are no specialists on the soccer field. Each player must be able to play a role in both defense and attack. And although soccer players don't have to be any particular size or shape, all must have a high level of fitness and athleticism. Field players may run several miles during the course of a match, much of that distance at sprintlike speed. The physical and mental challenges confronting players are many and great. Individual and team performance ultimately depends on each player's ability to meet these challenges.

Once considered a "foreign" sport by North Americans, among team sports in the United States today soccer is second only to basketball in the number of participants. Participation in youth soccer continues to grow internationally as an increasing number of boys and girls ages 6 to 18 are playing the game each year. The expanding pool of players at all age levels has, in turn, created a need for more soccer coaches. While some may have grown up playing the game, many are volunteers with little or no playing experience in the sport and even less experience teaching the game to youngsters. As a consequence, coaches new to the game are faced with what would appear to be an overwhelming challenge as they try to provide a good training environment for their respective teams. In reality, however, despite having had little or no exposure to the sport when they were younger, many of today's youth coaches are outstanding. They have become excellent teachers of the game by educating themselves, attending clinics, participating in coaching courses, reading books, and watching high-level soccer games. *Soccer Practice Games* will add to their body of knowledge.

Novice and experienced coaches alike are constantly searching for innovative exercises to use in their practice sessions. This third edition of *Soccer Practice Games* provides coaches with a variety of games designed to nurture the technical, tactical, and physical development of players. All exercises will challenge players and will keep them active, interested, and involved. The games are competitive and fun to play, and they can be easily adapted to a wide range of ages and abilities. Players of all ages respond more favorably if they are excited and enthusiastic about what they are doing—in short, if they are having a good time in the process. The games described here create such a positive training atmosphere. This does not imply that standard drills have no place in the team's practice regimen. The optimal learning environment should include a balance between typical soccer drills and the games found in this book.

As coaches, we should never underestimate the fundamental wisdom contained in the adage "The game is the best teacher." Many of the greatest players in soccer's rich history developed the foundation for their exceptional talent while playing in pick-up games, the so-called street soccer of their youth. Their eventual development into the best that soccer has to offer was not a direct result of years of training in a highly structured, coach-dominated practice routine, but rather from player-organized games in which the participants and the game itself were the dominant factors. Coaches never were and never should be the central driving force behind player development; rather, we should view ourselves as facilitators of such development. Toward that end, practices should be coach guided rather than coach directed. We can do so by providing players with practices that are game oriented, practices that constantly challenge them to take initiative and make decisions, and practices that ultimately encourage players to accept responsibility for their success. The games in this book will help you to create such a training atmosphere and, at the same time, provide players and coaches alike with an enjoyable and memorable experience.

Acknowledgments

The teamwork required in producing a successful soccer team can be likened to the collective effort that goes into the writing and publishing of a high-quality book. You simply cannot do it alone. In that regard, I am deeply indebted to many people for their help with this project. Although it is not possible to mention everyone by name, I would like to express my sincere appreciation to the following people:

The staff at Human Kinetics, particularly Carla Zych, offered valuable insight and advice in developing the book and finalizing the manuscript.

Tom Heine, acquisitions editor, was willing to consider the concept and initiate the process.

The staff coaches of Shoot to Score Soccer Academy shared their thoughts and ideas with me.

Special thanks go to the young soccer players who volunteered their time and effort to model many of the photos that accompany the text: Alexandra Davidson, Gabriella and Ronaldo Del Duca, Danny Ferris, Jonny Geisler, Jeff Howard, Eliza and Travis Luxbacher, Ethan Marsh, Meredith and Elizabeth McDonough, and Jonathan Pyles. I sincerely hope they continue to enjoy the game for many years to come.

My sincere appreciation is also extended to Tom Goodman, a valued member of the coaching fraternity, for his willingness to provide the foreword to *Soccer Practice Games*. Last but certainly not least, I want to thank my beautiful wife, Gail, the love of my life, for her support and encouragement of my many interests and projects.

Introduction: Make Practice Games Work for You

Planning a practice that challenges players to achieve a higher level of performance, a practice that motivates them to work hard, improve their game, and at the end of the day beg for more, is a fundamental responsibility of the soccer coach. Players of all ages and abilities want to be excited, enthusiastic, and active while they learn the game. Most will not respond well to long-winded lectures, standing in line, or anything that spells boredom. Young soccer players in particular will derive the most benefit from practices that are challenging and fun; from exercises that are activity oriented; from games in which they are constantly moving, touching the ball, and scoring goals. This third edition of *Soccer Practice Games* will assist you, as a coach, in achieving that goal.

The book contains 175 gamelike activities that you can use in creating a rich and varied practice environment. The practice games described in each chapter focus on mastery of the skills and tactics required for becoming a more complete soccer player. Players are placed in controlled, competitive situations that provide everyone involved with an opportunity to succeed. The games are particularly useful for beginning and intermediate players and can be easily adapted to accommodate more traditional training with older, more experienced players.

The book contains nine chapters, each with a specific theme. Chapter 1 explains how to best use the material presented in the book to organize good training sessions. Chapter 2 describes a variety of games that will physically and mentally prepare players for practice and match competition. Chapters 3 through 9 present games that deal with specific skills or tactical concepts (such as dribbling and shielding, passing and receiving). Although the games are categorized based on their primary focus, most actually emphasize two or more essential elements of the sport. For example, all the individual and small-group games in chapter 7 require players to rehearse tactical concepts while dribbling, passing, or receiving the ball as they move throughout the playing area, in some cases against challenging opponents. As a result, players can derive fitness, skill, and tactical benefits all within the same exercise. When possible, the games included in each chapter are loosely organized in a progression of increasing complexity. The ordering assists you in selecting games that are most appropriate for your players. Expose novice players to the most basic games first so that they are not overwhelmed and can achieve some degree of success. As players become more confident and competent, you can progress to more mentally and physically challenging situations. Experienced players will derive greater benefit from games that require them to perform under conditions that they will actually face in match situations, gamelike pressures that include limited space and time, physical fatigue, and challenging opponents.

Each game is categorized as beginning, intermediate, or advanced based on its perceived level of difficulty. Beginner games focus primarily on technique (skill) development. These exercises are competitive and fun to play, introduce players to the gamelike pressures of restricted space and limited time, and involve repetition of the specific skill coupled with player movement with and without the ball. Intermediate games also require players to execute skills under gamelike conditions but couple that aspect of performance with individual and group tactical play. These games are characterized by an increased emphasis on speed of repetition and speed of play. The pressure of challenging opponents is also introduced in some of these exercises, but to a limited extent only. Advanced games focus primarily on tactical development at the group and team level. Players must already have a fundamental mastery of all soccer skills in order to derive the greatest benefit from these exercises. Hence, these exercises are not appropriate for beginning or even intermediate performers. Games in this category are typically performed under match conditions in order to expose players to the actual pressures they will encounter in a competitive game. Such pressures involve increased physical demands, reduced time and space in which to execute skills and make tactical decisions, and the determined challenge of opponents competing for possession of the ball. Keep in mind that the categorization of games is somewhat subjective; most games are extremely versatile and, with a few minor adjustments, can usually be adapted to accommodate the age and the ability of players involved. For example, you can make a beginner game more challenging for your players by doing the following:

- Impose restrictions on players; for example, require one- or two-touch passing only, or designate a specific type of pass only.
- Manipulate the size of the playing area (reducing the area increases the degree of difficulty since players must perform the same skills in less time and space).
- Increase the physical demands of the game by requiring more running and player movement.
- Incorporate skill and tactical aspects into the same exercise; for example, require players to choose the best of several options when deciding when and where to pass the ball.
- Add the ultimate challenge—the pressure of determined opponents competing for the ball.

Best of all, whether the game is shaped to test the novice or challenge the experienced player, it remains fast-paced and functional for everyone involved. Each game is organized in an easily understood format, as the following describes:

Title. In most cases, but not all, the title provides a general idea of what the game involves and emphasizes. For example, Dribble the Maze and Score requires players to dribble through and around obstacles before shooting on goal. Some titles are not as obvious, however, and you should look to other headings, such as objectives, for more information on the game's utility.

Difficulty rating. Beginning, intermediate, or advanced levels are indicated by soccer ball icons. Beginning games are identified by a single soccer ball icon, intermediate games by two soccer balls, and advanced games with three soccer balls.

Minutes. A suggested time frame is provided for each game. This is offered as a general guideline only and should be adjusted according to the age, ability, and physical maturity of players involved. The duration of a game is ultimately your decision as the coach, because you know the needs and abilities of your players better than anyone else.

Players. Some games require a specific number of players while others do not. For example, Playing the Wall requires 3 players because the entire focus is on the 2v1 situation. Other games, such as Chain Gang or Connect the Dots, can involve a range of players. When determining how many players to include in a game, keep in mind that all should be active throughout the exercise and touching the ball most of the time. When too many players are involved, or too few balls are available, the game will not accomplish its objectives.

Objectives. Most games have a primary objective and two or more closely associated secondary objectives. For example, the primary emphasis of the game Tackle All Balls is on the development of dribbling skills used for possessing and protecting the ball in tight spaces. Secondary objectives include the development of shielding and tackling skills as well as an improved level of fitness. Using games that accomplish more than one objective makes the best use of limited practice time and is commonly referred to as economical training.

You should take into consideration a game's primary objective to determine whether it fits into the general theme of the specific practice. For example, if the central theme of a training session is the improvement of passing and receiving skills, then the games selected for that specific practice should fit that criterion.

Setup. Field dimensions, equipment, and any other special needs are listed under this heading. The field dimensions shown are provided as approximate guidelines, and therefore coaches can substitute meters for yards. Balls, cones, flags, and colored scrimmage vests are some of the most common equipment items. Field dimensions are provided only as general guidelines and should be adjusted to suit the age, number, and ability of players.

Procedure. This section contains an overview of how the game is played. For some games, coaches may act as servers or scorekeepers while observing the action, but that is not always necessary. The majority of games are designed so that players can use their own initiative and decision-making ability to organize the action and get play started.

Scoring. When appropriate, a scoring system has been provided to add an element of competition to the game. It should be clearly understood, however, that the ultimate aim of each game is for players to challenge themselves to achieve a higher standard of performance. Improvement is the true barometer of success, not who wins or loses the practice game.

Practice tips. These suggestions help you organize the games in the most efficient and effective manner. Most deal with possible adjustments in the size of the playing area or with restrictions placed on the players (for instance, one- or two-touch passing). Safety and liability concerns are also addressed when appropriate.

As the coach you are ultimately responsible for creating an exciting learning environment for your players. The games that follow should assist you in achieving that objective. Each game can, with subtle variations, be shaped to match the physical and mental maturity of the players under your charge. Your players will be challenged to improve their performance and will have an enjoyable time in the process—and so will you.

Key to Diagrams

- - - - →   Path of ball

〰〰〰→   Dribble

——→   Path of player

——»»→   Shot

⚑   Flag

△   Cone

⚽   Ball

CHAPTER 1

Planning Practice Sessions

One of your most important responsibilities as coach is to consider the abilities of the players under your charge and then plan an appropriate training program. Young players are not miniature adults, so a training session that is spot on for a college-aged team might be totally inappropriate for players 10 and younger. Evaluate your players' level of skill (if any!), tactical knowledge, fitness, and physical maturity and develop a practice that will keep everyone active and involved. Activities shouldn't be too physically or technically difficult to perform, but they should require players to extend themselves in order to achieve a higher standard of performance. That is the art of coaching—planning a good practice session that is tailored to the strengths and weaknesses of your specific group.

The following general guidelines apply to players of all ages and ability levels and will assist you in planning practice sessions. These are suggestions only and should be adapted to accommodate the specific needs of individual players and teams.

Create a positive learning atmosphere. Regardless of whether you are introducing the sport to a group of youngsters or attempting to fine-tune a team of grizzled professionals, a boring practice equates with a poor learning environment. While practices should be demanding, organized, and focused, they should also provide an enjoyable experience for players and coaches alike. Keep players active, involved, touching the ball, and scoring goals.

Through careful planning and creative thinking, you can provide stimulating, highly motivated training sessions guaranteed to meet your specific learning objectives.

Develop a theme. Don't attempt to cover too many topics in a single practice session, particularly with younger players. Plan each practice around a central theme. For example, the primary focus of a training session could be to improve passing and receiving skills or to create goal-scoring opportunities through creative dribbling. Organize the practice around a variety of exercises and practice games related to the central theme.

Take into account your players' soccer age. A player's "soccer age" refers to level of competence. In many cases a player's soccer age may differ significantly from chronological age. Novice players who have never touched a soccer ball are developmentally behind players of the same age who have played the game for several years. In short, the experienced player has a more advanced soccer age. Beginning players may have difficulty executing even the most fundamental skills, so you should not place them in situations where they have little or no chance of achieving some degree of success. Your goal is to plan a realistic practice, one that challenges players but is also within their physical and mental capabilities. Consider players' technical abilities (that is, skill), physical maturity, and developmental level, and then develop a practice appropriate for that specific group.

No lines, no lectures. The more times a player can pass, receive, shoot, head, or dribble the ball, the more likely he will enjoy the practice and at the same time improve his skill level. Conversely, standing in long lines while listening to the coach talk and waiting for an infrequent opportunity to touch the ball doesn't make for a good practice. Make sure that a large supply of balls, ideally one for each player, is available. An ample supply of balls provides you with many more choices of activities and practice games and makes training more enjoyable for the players since they are constantly moving and touching the ball. The easiest way to guarantee a sufficient number of balls is to require each player to bring a ball to practice. Just as baseball players bring their glove to the field, soccer players should bring a ball.

Keep the session simple. Much of soccer's inherent beauty rests with the fact that it is basically a simple game. Keep it that way! Complicated drills and highly intricate training exercises will serve only to confuse and frustrate players rather than motivate them. When planning practices, always take into consideration the KISS principle of coaching—keep it simple, stupid! This principle applies to coaching all ages and ability levels.

Teach in a progression. Planning an effective practice requires much more thought than simply selecting a bunch of unrelated activities and haphazardly using them during a training session. Each practice game should lay the groundwork for those that follow. Introduce the session with basic activities, and progress to more matchlike situations. For example, the practice might begin with simple passing games involving minimal player movement and gradually progress to exercises where players must pass and receive the ball while moving at game speed under the pressure of challenging opponents. The starting point in the progression depends on the ability and experience of the players. Higher-level players will naturally begin with more demanding exercises than novice players will. In both cases, however, organize the sequence of practice games so that each serves as a natural lead-in for the next. Each game should relate to the central theme of the practice session.

Keep it player centered. Practice should be player centered, not coach centered. Introduce the topic, use brief demonstrations and simple explanations, and then get the players actively involved as soon as possible. Avoid long stretches of inactivity—the less time players stand or sit around, the better the practice. You can stop the action at opportune times to make a coaching point or to provide specific and appropriate feedback.

Ensure a safe training environment. Soccer is a contact sport, and as such it involves a certain amount of physical risk. Accidental collisions, bumps, and bruises sometimes occur. To minimize injuries, make every effort to provide players with a safe practice and playing environment. This includes supervising and planning, matching players with others of similar size and ability, and establishing guidelines for appropriate behavior.

Players must wear appropriate equipment during practice and games. Both field players and goalkeepers should wear shin guards to prevent lower-leg injuries. Most guards are made of light, flexible plastic and are relatively inexpensive. Goalkeepers should wear position-specific equipment as well. Padded shorts or full-length pants are recommended, particularly when training and playing on hard natural surfaces or artificial turf. Both shorts and pants have padding over the hip area. Gloves are also an important part of the goalkeeper's equipment. Young goalkeepers should wear padded helmets when playing indoor soccer to lessen the incidence of head injuries.

Take special care when selecting and securing soccer goals. Despite their heavy weight, portable full-size goals (8 feet high by 24 feet wide) can topple over if not properly anchored, particularly when there are strong winds or if players hang on the crossbar. Solid, professionally made goals firmly secured to the ground are recommended, but they are also expensive. If cost is an issue, and for most of us it is, you can position cones, flags, or other kinds of markers to represent goals. Many youth-size goals can be safely anchored with sand bags placed at appropriate places.

Practice economical training. Many coaches have only one or two practice sessions a week with their team, in addition to the game, so it is difficult to cover everything you would like to do in the time allotted. To make the most effective use of limited practice time, you should incorporate, when possible, the elements of fitness, skill, and tactics into each activity. Toward that end, try to include a ball in every exercise, even those designed primarily to improve fitness. However long the practice session, make sure that the time is well spent. The quality of training is much more important than the quantity of training.

End with a game. Above all else, soccer players want to play the game. Reward their hard work by ending each training session with a game or a game simulation. The match need not be a full-sided (11v11) affair. Small-sided games (3v3 up to 6v6) are actually more beneficial in many respects. Playing with fewer members per team allows players a greater opportunity to pass, receive, dribble, and shoot the ball. Small-sided competitions also require players to make more decisions because they are directly involved in virtually every play, a situation that promotes tactical development. The emphasis on positional play is also greatly reduced since each player must defend as well as attack, a situation that promotes total-player development. Last but not least, the number of scoring chances is greatly increased in small-sided games, and this makes the practice more fun for everyone involved. Keep in mind that making mistakes and learning from errors are important parts of the learning process, so players should be encouraged to take risks and to experiment with what works and what doesn't. You can briefly stop play and correct mistakes at appropriate times during the games.

Evaluate the session. At the conclusion of each practice, it's a good idea to reflect on how things went during that particular session. Were the players having fun? Was the practice too long—did the players lose interest? Was it too short—were they asking for more? Did each player get ample touches on the ball? Were all players provided an opportunity to play in both attacking and defending roles? Did all players have repeated opportunities to go to goal? Answering these and similar questions will enable you to adjust your practices accordingly to create the best possible learning environment for player development.

CHAPTER 2

Warm-Up and Conditioning Games

A thorough warm-up performed before each practice and game prepares players for the more vigorous activity to follow. Warm-up activities raise muscle temperatures and increase suppleness, promote increased blood flow and oxygen supply, improve muscular contraction and reflex time, and minimize muscle strains and next-day soreness. The duration of a warm-up can vary from one training session to the next and from one team to another, depending on individual needs. Generally, the warm-up should be of sufficient duration and intensity to induce sweating, an indicator that muscle temperatures have been elevated. This could take anywhere from 15 to 30 minutes, depending on the ambient temperature, humidity, and general environmental conditions. Obviously, players won't have to warm up as hard or as long on a hot, humid summer day as they will on a cold, blustery winter evening.

Any form of activity that involves repeated action of large muscle groups can be used in the warm-up. Traditional exercises include a variety of stretches coupled with old favorites such as jumping jacks, sit-ups, push-ups, and knee bends. This type of warm-up is commonly referred to as an unrelated warm-up because it does not involve soccer-specific movements like passing, dribbling, and shooting the ball. While nothing is inherently wrong with an unrelated warm-up, most players prefer a soccer-related warm-up, which is more appropriate from both a mental and physical perspective. A soccer-related warm-up can include skill-related games that use passing or dribbling skills, or it can take the form of games that stress the movements, mobility, and agility required of players in a soccer match. The games described in this chapter add variety and enjoyment to the team warm-up while at the same time achieving the primary objective of preparing players for the vigorous training to follow. Many of the games (though not all) require players to pass, shoot, or dribble one or more soccer balls, so skill development is an added benefit of these games.

To a certain extent, physical conditioning can also be maintained, and in some cases improved, through many of the games described in this chapter. For example, tag games can improve both aerobic and anaerobic endurance while developing additional components of soccer-specific fitness such as agility, mobility, and balance. Other games focus more on muscular strength, speed, and power. Players can improve soccer-specific speed by performing exercises that require sudden changes of speed and direction along with deceptive body movements. Quickness, balance, and an ability to suddenly change direction are as important to a soccer player as straight-out sprinting speed.

Minutes: 10

Players: Unlimited

Objectives: To improve mobility and agility; to improve communication; to develop endurance

Setup: Use markers to outline a 30-yard square. Designate two players as It and have them stand outside the area. Have all remaining free players stand within the square.

Procedure: The players who are It enter the area to chase after and tag free players. Free players are allowed to move anywhere within the field area to avoid being tagged. A free player who is tagged must join hands with the player who tagged her to form a chain. As more players are tagged, the chains grow longer. Only two chains are permitted at any one time (the original chains may not split into smaller chains). Chains can work together to corner or trap free players. Continue until only two free players remain. Repeat the game, with those two players being It to begin the next round.

Scoring: The last two remaining free players win the game.

Practice tips: Vary the size of the area or the number of chains allowed depending on the number of players. Free players should use sudden changes of speed and direction coupled with deceptive body feints to avoid being tagged.

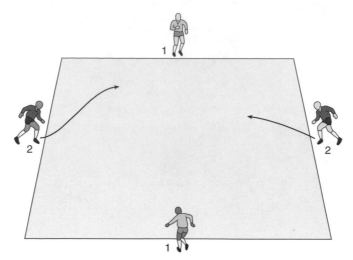

2 Hounds and Hares ⚽

Minutes: 10

Players: Unlimited, organized into groups of 4 (2 hounds, 2 hares)

Objective: To develop mobility, agility, and deceptive body feints; to improve aerobic fitness

Setup: Each group plays within a 15-yard square. Arrange players into pairs and assign each pair a number (1 and 2). One player from each group stands on each sideline of the square with the partners directly opposite each other. One partner is designated the hound and the other is the hare to begin the game. No balls are required.

Procedure: Begin the game by calling out a number, such as 1. The number 1 players immediately enter the square, and the hound gives chase in an attempt to catch (tag) the hare. If the hare is tagged, players reverse roles immediately. Play continuously for 60 seconds, and then send the other pair into the square to play while the initial hound and hare return to their original positions on the perimeter and rest.

Scoring: None

Practice tips: This is a physically demanding game when played at full intensity. The hare should use quick changes of speed and direction to elude the hound. Make the game more challenging by lengthening the duration of each round or increasing the size of the square. As a variation, call two or three pairs into the circle at the same time.

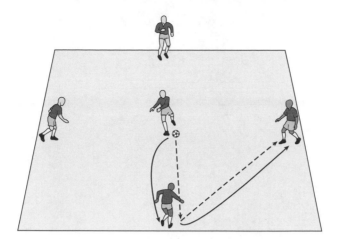

Minutes: 10

Players: 5

Objective: To develop the ability to receive and pass the ball using only two touches; to increase sprinting speed

Setup: Use markers to outline a 20-yard square. Station one player at the midpoint of each sideline. Station the fifth player in the center of the square with the ball.

Procedure: To begin, the central player passes the ball to one of the sideline players and sprints to that receiver's spot. The sideline player receives and prepares the ball with the first touch, passes to another player with the second touch, and sprints to that spot. Players continue passing and following the pass at maximum speed.

Scoring: None

Practice tips: Emphasize a good first touch; the ball should be controlled and prepared with the first touch and then passed to a teammate with the second touch. Encourage players to make hard sprints in support of their pass, just as they would in a game situation.

Minutes: 15 to 20 minutes

Players: Unlimited (15 or more players preferred)

Objectives: To improve dribbling, passing, agility, and mobility; to encourage teamwork

Setup: Outline a playing area at least 50 yards square. Divide the group into three teams of equal numbers. Use cones or discs to designate a 15-yard square as home base for each team; each team's base is located in a different area of the field. All players, each with a ball, begin play standing in their team's home base. In addition, each team designates one of its members as the team doctor. The team doctor also stands within the team base but does not have a ball.

Procedure: On the command to begin, all players except the team doctor immediately leave their home base to dribble after players from other teams. The objective is for the dribblers to contact opponents below the knees with a passed ball. A player who is contacted with a ball passed by an opponent is frozen and must take a knee at that spot. Frozen players can only be released by their team doctor, who must leave the team's home base to tag frozen teammates. Once tagged by their doctor, frozen players are released to dribble after opponents. The team doctor is safe when stationed within the team's home base but is fair game when outside of the home base. If the doctor is hit with a passed ball when attempting to unfreeze teammates, then he is permanently frozen and from that point on the players from that team who are frozen cannot be released. Play a series of 5-minute games.

Scoring: The team that has the fewest players frozen at the end of the round wins. Play several rounds; the team winning the most rounds wins the game.

Practice tips: Reduce the area size to make it easier for the passers to hit their targets.

Minutes: 10

Players: Unlimited

Objective: To develop dribbling skills; to encourage competitiveness

Setup: Play within the penalty area. Each player tucks a colored flag into the back of her shorts. At least half the flag should be hanging out. Each player has a ball.

Procedure: Players begin dribbling among themselves within the penalty area. On your command, the game begins. Players dribble after other players and try to steal their flags while also keeping their own flags safe from other players. Players should keep a flag tucked into the back of their shorts while holding stolen flags in their hand as they dribble about. Players should dribble the ball under close control at all times and are not permitted to leave the ball to chase after an opponent. Play several games.

Scoring: The player who ends up with the most stolen flags while retaining her own flag wins the game.

Practice tips: As a variation, have players perform a dribbling move (such as a step-over or a chop) after they steal an opponent's flag.

⑥ Dribble Relay ⚽

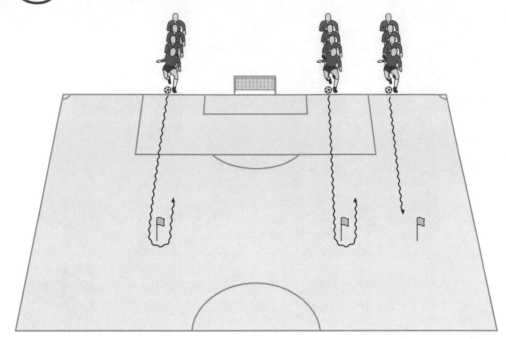

Minutes: 10

Players: Unlimited (equal-sized teams of 4 to 6)

Objectives: To develop dribbling speed; to improve fitness

Setup: Use the end line of the field as a starting line. Have players on each team line up single file and stand side by side with the other teams behind the starting line, with at least three yards between teams. Place a marker 25 yards at the front and center of each team. The first player in line for each team has a ball.

Procedure: On command, the first player dribbles as fast as possible around the marker and back to the start line where he exchanges the ball with the next player in line. That player in turn dribbles around the marker and back to the start line, and exchanges possession with the next player in line. Continue until all team members have completed the circuit. The team completing the relay in the shortest time wins. Repeat 10 times with a short rest between each race.

Scoring: The winning team gets 3 points, second place 2 points, and third place 1 point. The team totaling the most points after 10 races wins the event.

Practice tips: The technique a player uses to dribble in open space differs from that used when dribbling for close control. When in open space, players should push the ball several steps ahead with the outside surface of the foot, sprint to catch up to it, and push it again. As they near the marker, they must keep the ball closer to their feet as they dribble around it, and then quickly shift gears into speed dribble mode as they return to the start line. Adjust the total distance covered to accommodate the age and fitness level of players.

Minutes: 5

Players: Unlimited

Objectives: To improve agility, mobility, and creative running; to generate enthusiasm and enjoyment

Setup: Use markers to outline a 40-yard-square playing area. No balls required.

Procedure: All players stand within the field area. Designate two pairs of twins who hold hands; all other (free) players do not pair up. On your command, the game begins. The twins attempt to tag the free players. A free player who is tagged joins the twin's chain. When the chain grows to include four players, the original twins drop off and become free players, and the new twins attempt to chase and tag free players in order to become free themselves.

Scoring: None

Practice tips: To make the game more difficult, require the free players to dribble soccer balls as they try to evade being tagged by the twins.

8) Dribble the Gauntlet ⚽

Minutes: 10 to 15

Players: Unlimited

Objective: To develop passing and dribbling skills; to improve mobility, agility, and fitness

Setup: Use markers to outline an area 25 yards wide by 40 yards long, with a safety zone 5 yards deep at each end. Station three marksmen in the center of the field, each with a ball. All remaining players, each with a ball, stand in a safety zone facing the marksmen.

Procedure: On your command, the players in the safety zone attempt to dribble the length of the field into the opposite safety zone. Marksmen capture the dribblers by contacting them below the knees with a passed ball. All passes must be made with the inside or outside surface of the foot; no shooting is permitted. A dribbler who is contacted below the knees with a passed ball, or who loses control of her ball outside the field boundaries, is considered captured and joins the marksmen for the next round. Dribblers who reach the safety zone remain there until the command to return to the original safety zone. Players dribble back and forth between safety zones until all but three have been captured. These players are marksmen for the next game.

Scoring: The last three players to avoid capture are the winners.

Practice tips: Adjust the area to match the ages, abilities, and number of players. Encourage marksmen to dribble close to their targets before passing the ball.

Minutes: 3 per round (several rounds)

Players: Unlimited

Objective: To sharpen dribbling skills; to improve agility and mobility with the ball

Setup: Use markers to outline an area 25 yards wide by 30 yards long. Designate two players as chasers, who stand outside the area without balls. All remaining players (free players) stand within the playing area, each with a ball.

Procedure: Free players dribble randomly within the area. On command, the two chasers enter the area and attempt to tag the free players, who must continue to dribble the ball while trying to evade the chasers. A player who is tagged is considered frozen and must sit on his ball. Free players can release teammates who are frozen by dribbling close and touching them on the shoulder. Continue for 3 minutes or until all players are frozen, whichever comes first. Repeat the game several times, with different chasers for each game.

Scoring: The chaser gets 1 point for each player tagged. The chaser who scores the most points wins the round.

Practice tips: This is an excellent dribbling exercise for beginning players. Adjust the size of the playing area to accommodate the ages and number of your players. Older players will need more space than younger players.

Minutes: 5

Players: Unlimited (in pairs)

Objectives: To develop dribbling skills; to improve quickness

Setup: Use markers to outline a large playing area (size depends on the number of participating players). Players partner up with a teammate; all but two pairs have a soccer ball to begin.

Procedure: Partners hold hands as they dribble the ball randomly within the area, exchanging possession of the ball every few seconds. The two pairs without a ball, the sharks, also hold hands, jogging within the area and cruising around the dribblers in preparation of stealing a ball. On the command of "Shark attack," each of the dribbling pairs leaves the ball and attempt to find a different ball. The sharks immediately secure a free ball and become dribblers. The two pairs of players left without a ball become sharks for the next round.

Scoring: None

Practice tips: Encourage dribblers to keep the ball under close control and encourage partners to exchange possession of the ball every few seconds.

Minutes: 10 to 15

Players: 12 to 16 (4 equal-sized teams)

Objective: To develop dribbling skills; to improve mobility, agility, and fitness

Setup: Use markers to outline a playing area 25 yards by 40 yards. Have all four teams stand in the field area, each player with a ball. Designate one team as It. Use colored scrimmage vests to differentiate teams.

Procedure: Players on the It team chase and attempt to tag players from the other three teams. All players, including the chasers, must dribble balls as they move within the field area. Players who are It are not permitted to leave their balls when attempting to tag opponents—they must dribble the ball under close control at all times. Any player tagged leaves the field to practice juggling. The game ends when all opponents have been eliminated or after 4 minutes, whichever comes first. Play four games, designating a different team as chasers for each game.

Scoring: The team that eliminates all its opponents in the least amount of time wins the competition.

Practice tips: Reduce the field area for younger players.

(12) Toss to Target ⚽⚽

Minutes: 10 to 15

Players: 12 to 20 (2 equal-sized teams of 6 to 10)

Objectives: To improve endurance; to rehearse the support movement required to create successful passing combinations

Setup: Use markers to outline an area 40 yards wide by 50 yards long. Divide the group into two teams of equal number. Use colored scrimmage vests to differentiate teams. Have both teams stand within the area. Designate one player on each team as a target, who wears distinctive clothing (hat, shirt, or vest). Award one team possession of the ball to begin.

Procedure: Teammates pass the ball among themselves by throwing (and catching) it—not by kicking it. The objective is to contact the opposing target below the knees with a thrown ball. The target is free to move anywhere within the area to avoid being hit. A player is permitted three or fewer steps with the ball before releasing it to a teammate or throwing at the target. Teammates can protect their target by blocking or deflecting opponent's throws. Change of possession occurs when a pass is intercepted by a member of the opposing team, the ball drops to the ground, or a player takes too many steps with the ball. Players may not wrestle the ball from an opponent.

Scoring: A team scores 1 point each time a player hits the opposing target below the knees with a thrown ball. The team scoring the most points wins.

Practice tips: As a variation, have two balls in play at the same time. Encourage short, accurate passes (tosses) with a high likelihood of completion. Attacking players should continually adjust their positions to provide multiple passing options for the teammate with the ball. Repeat the game several times, with different players serving as the targets.

Minutes: 12 (4 periods of 3 minutes each)

Players: Unlimited (2 equal-sized teams)

Objectives: To practice making sudden changes of direction while dribbling the ball; to improve the ability to dribble for close control in a confined area; to foster the competitive spirit

Setup: Use markers to outline an area 25 yards wide by 30 yards long. Have the players on team 1 stand as stationary targets at various spots within the playing area with feet planted and spread apart. Team 2 players, each with a ball, start outside the area.

Procedure: On command, team 2 players dribble into the area and attempt to push (pass) their ball through the legs of as many team 1 players as possible during a 3-minute round. The maneuver of pushing the ball through an opponent's legs is called a nutmeg and, in actual game competition, is the ultimate embarrassment for a defender. Team 1 players must remain stationary during the 3-minute round. A dribbler may not nutmeg the same opponent twice in succession. Teams reverse roles for the second round and for each successive round. Play at least four rounds.

Scoring: Players compete using the honor system to tally scores. Each player counts the number of nutmegs she performs in the allotted time. Teammates total their scores after the round. The team with the most nutmegs after four rounds wins the game.

Practice tips: Adjust the size of the playing area to accommodate the number of players. To avoid collisions, stationary players should not stand too close together among dribblers.

(14) Pinball Possession ⚽⚽

Minutes: 10

Players: 5 to 8 (1 defender; the remaining players are attackers)

Objectives: To develop one-touch passing ability; to improve mobility, agility, change of pace; to warm up players before moving to more vigorous training

Setup: Use markers to form a circle about 12 yards in diameter. One player stands as a defender within the circle; position the other players evenly spaced along the perimeter as attackers. One attacker has a ball to begin.

Procedure: Attackers attempt to keep the ball from the defender by passing among themselves. Attackers are permitted to move laterally along the perimeter of the circle to receive a passed ball but may not move into the circle. Attackers must execute only one-touch passes through the circle (thus the name, pinball soccer) and then immediately follow their passes to a position at that spot on the circle. If the ball goes out of the circle because of an errant pass, or if the defender intercepts a pass, the ball is immediately returned to an attacker, and the game continues.

Scoring: Award the attackers 1 point for 8 consecutive passes without a loss of possession. Award the defender 1 point for stealing the ball and for each time the ball goes out of the circle. Play to 8 points; then switch defenders. Repeat until each player has played as the defender.

Practice tips: To make the game more challenging for advanced players, have two defenders in the circle. For less skilled players, enlarge the circle and permit two-touch passing.

Minutes: 3 per round (repeated several times)

Players: 11 to 20

Objective: To develop dribbling skills; to create an enjoyable training atmosphere

Setup: Use markers to outline a rectangular area 20 yards by 30 yards. Designate four players to be crabs, who start within the play area. Crabs must move about in a crabwalk (a sitting position with weight supported by hands and feet). Remaining players begin outside the area, each with a ball.

Procedure: On command, the players outside the area enter to dribble among the crabs. The crabs crawl after the dribblers and attempt to kick the balls out of the area. Crabs must move about in the crab position and may not use their hands to play the ball. Dribblers use quick changes of speed and direction, coupled with deceptive body feints, to elude the crabs. Crabs can work together to reduce the space available to dribblers and force them into errors. A player whose ball is kicked out of the area becomes a crab, so the number of crabs continues to increase as the game progresses. Continue until all but four dribblers have been eliminated. Repeat the game with those four players as crabs.

Scoring: Crabs score 1 point for each ball kicked out of the area. The crab with the most points wins.

Practice tips: To make the game more challenging, reduce the area size or increase the number of crabs. Caution dribblers not to step on the crabs' hands.

16 Sharks and Minnows ⚽⚽

Minutes: 10 to 15

Players: Unlimited

Objective: To rehearse dribbling and tackling skills; to improve mobility, agility, and fitness

Setup: Use markers to outline an area 20 yards wide by 30 yards long, with a safety zone 3 yards wide at each end spanning the width of the field. Designate three or four players to be sharks who stand, without balls, in the center of the playing area. Remaining players (minnows) begin play in one of the safety zones, each with a ball.

Procedure: On command, the minnows attempt to dribble (swim) the length of the playing area into the opposite safety zone. Sharks try to prevent this by kicking the minnows' balls out of the area. A minnow whose ball is kicked out of the area becomes a shark for the next round. Minnows who dribble from one safety zone into the other remain there until all fellow minnows have arrived; at this point, issue the command to return to the original safety zone. Minnows continue dribbling back and forth, from one safety zone to the other, on your command. Continue the game until all but three minnows have been eliminated. These three players are sharks to begin the next game.

Scoring: None

Practice tips: Reduce the field width to make the game more challenging for the minnows.

Minutes: 10 to 15

Players: 12 to 20 (3 hunters; the remaining players are rabbits)

Objectives: To hone passing and dribbling skills; to improve agility and mobility with the ball

Setup: Use markers to outline a field area 30 yards wide by 40 yards long. Designate three players as hunters, who stand outside the area, each with a ball. Remaining players, the rabbits, start within the area without balls. A supply of balls, one for each rabbit, is placed outside of the playing area.

Procedure: At your command, the hunters enter the area to dribble after and contact rabbits below the knees with a passed ball. Rabbits may move anywhere within the area to avoid being hit. Any rabbit contacted by a ball below the knee immediately collects one of the loose balls placed outside of the area and joins the hunt. Continue play until all rabbits have been eliminated. Repeat several times, using different hunters to begin each game.

Scoring: None

Practice tips: Adjust the area size to accommodate the ages, abilities, and number of players. Encourage hunters to dribble close to their targets before passing. This helps develop dribbling skills and also increases the likelihood of an accurate pass. As a variation, require hunters to use a specific type of pass (such as an inside-of-foot or instep pass only) or have them use their nondominant foot to pass the ball.

(18) Team Handball ⚽ ⚽

Minutes: 15

Players: 12 to 20 (2 equal-sized teams)

Objectives: To simulate the support movement used in actual match situations; to improve mobility, agility, and fitness

Setup: Use markers to create a playing area 40 yards wide by 60 yards long, with a small goal positioned in the center of each end line. Organize two teams of equal size. Use colored vests to differentiate teams. You'll need one ball per game. No goalies.

Procedure: Each team defends a goal. Players pass by throwing (and catching) rather than kicking the ball; otherwise, regular soccer rules apply. Players may take up to three steps with the ball before releasing it to a teammate or throwing it (shooting) at the goal. Change of possession occurs when the ball drops to the ground, a pass is intercepted, or a goal is scored. Players may not wrestle the ball from an opponent. Since there are no designated goalkeepers, all players are permitted to use their hands to block opponents' shots at goal.

Scoring: A goal is scored by throwing the ball into the opponent's goal. The team scoring the most goals wins the game.

Practice tips: Encourage teammates to attack as one compact unit, getting into positions at the proper angle and distance of support in relation to the player with the ball. Older players can have two balls in play at the same time.

Minutes: 5 to 10

Players: Unlimited

Objective: To rehearse the takeover maneuver (possession exchange) with a teammate; to improve fitness

Setup: Use markers to outline a rectangular area 25 wide by 30 yards long. All players start within the area, with one ball for every two players.

Procedure: On command, all players begin to move randomly throughout the playing area. Those with a ball dribble; those without a ball jog at one-half to three-quarter speed. The dribblers' goal is to exchange possession of the ball with one of the free players, using the takeover maneuver. Players should always execute the same foot takeover—if a player has the ball on her right foot, then the teammate taking the ball does so with her right foot. Same procedure applies when ball is on left foot.

Scoring: Players are awarded 1 point for each takeover with a teammate. Perform as many takeovers as possible in time allotted.

Practice tips: Teammates communicate with each other through verbal signals or subtle body movements. When executing the takeover, the player with the ball should dribble directly at a teammate while controlling the ball with the foot farthest from an imaginary defender. As players cross paths, they execute the takeover maneuver and exchange possession of the ball. To make the game more difficult, add one or two passive defenders to the exercise.

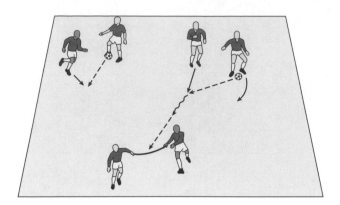

Minutes: 10

Players: Unlimited (in pairs)

Objectives: To practice dribbling and passing skills with a partner in order to move the ball into position to pass through a mobile goal

Setup: Use markers to outline a 30-yard-square playing area. Partner each player with a teammate; provide one ball per pair. Designate one pair as the mobile goal; this pair does not have a ball and moves throughout the area while holding opposite ends of a rope 4 yards long.

Procedure: The goal moves continuously and randomly throughout the area; at all times the rope should be stretched to its full length of 4 yards. Remaining pairs, each with a ball, attempt to move the ball by dribbling and passing into a position to pass through (beneath) the moving goal.

Scoring: Partners score 1 point for each pass through the mobile goal. The first pair to total of 5 points wins the game. Repeat the game with a different pair serving as the goal.

Practice tips: This game may be too difficult for young or inexperienced players who do not have fundamental passing and receiving skills. To simplify the game for younger or less experienced players, have two coaches or parents, rather than players, hold a 5-yard-long rope to create a wider mobile goal.

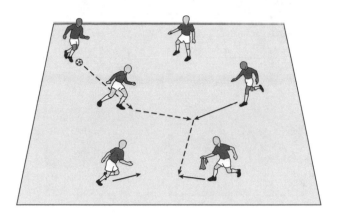

Minutes: 10

Players: 6 (1 target, 5 passers)

Objectives: To improve passing and receiving skills; to improve mobility, agility, and fitness

Setup: Outline a 15-yard-square field area. One ball is required; place a few extra balls outside the field area in case the ball leaves the area.

Procedure: Designate one player as the target; this player will hold a distinctive-colored shirt or vest in his hand. The remaining players team up to circulate the ball using two-touch passes and attempt to hit the target below the knees with a passed ball. Passers are restricted to two touches to pass and receive the ball as they move the ball into position to hit the target. If the target is hit with a passed ball, he immediately drops the colored vest, and the nearest player picks it up and becomes the target. Play continues for 10 minutes or more.

Scoring: None

Practice tips: Add variations to the game, such as requiring the passer to use his weakest foot to pass to hit the target, or possibly require the target to skip around the area to evade being hit by a passed ball.

Minutes: 5 to 10 continuous

Players: 16 to 20 (4 equal-sized teams plus 2 catchers)

Objectives: To improve fitness; to practice dribbling skills; to develop field awareness

Setup: Use markers to outline a 30-yard-square playing area. In each corner of the field, designate a 5-yard square as a base. Choose two catchers without soccer balls to stand in the center of the large square. Divide the other players into four equal-sized groups and have each group stand in one of the four corner squares. One soccer ball is required for each player.

Procedure: On the command of "Play ball," the game begins. Players standing on a base (base runners) must dribble to another base before being tagged out by a catcher. If a base runner gets to another base before being tagged, she is safe, but she may remain on that base for only five or fewer seconds before trying to reach another base. A base runner who is tagged immediately becomes a catcher; the previous catcher takes the ball and becomes a base runner. No more than four base runners can occupy a base at any one time, so if the base is filled, the other base runners must try to make it safely to another base.

Scoring: None

Practice tips: To make the game more difficult for the catchers, you can require the base runners to hang a flag or scrimmage vest out of the back of their shorts and then require the catcher to grab the flag or vest and pull it out rather than simply tagging the base runner.

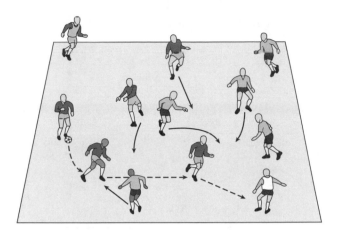

Minutes: 10

Players: Unlimited (2 equal-sized teams)

Objectives: To learn to work with teammates to move the ball into position to pass and hit a designated target (coyote) on the opposite team

Setup: Outline a playing area of approximately 30 yards by 30 yards. Divide the group into two teams of equal numbers; designate one player on each team as the coyote. The coyote wears a distinctive vest to differentiate him from his teammates. One ball is required.

Procedure: One team is awarded the ball to begin. Teammates dribble and pass among themselves in order to move the ball into a position where a player can contact the opponent's coyote with a passed ball. Coyotes are free to move throughout the area in an attempt to avoid being hit with a passed ball. Change of possession occurs when an opposing player intercepts a passed ball or when a coyote has been hit by a passed ball.

Scoring: Teams score 1 point for each time they hit the opponents' coyote with a passed ball. The team scoring the most points wins the game.

Practice tips: Encourage players to move the ball quickly into position to pass and hit the opposing coyote. Emphasize proper pace and accuracy of passes coupled with proper support positioning. Put two balls in play at one time for older, more experienced players.

Minutes: 10 to 15

Players: Unlimited (3 equal-sized teams)

Objectives: To move the ball quickly throughout the area by passing among teammates; to improve mobility, agility, and fitness

Setup: Use markers to outline a 35-yard-square playing area. Divide the group into three teams of relatively equal numbers. Each team has a ball to begin.

Procedure: Designate one team as the hunters who pass among themselves by throwing and catching the ball. The remaining two teams use only their feet to pass and receive their ball (i.e., their fish), attempting to move throughout the area quickly so that the hunters cannot hit their fish with a thrown ball. Players from all three teams are permitted to pass to and receive the ball from their teammates only, and not from players from the other team. Hunters are permitted three steps when in possession of the ball, after which they must release the ball (throw) to a teammate as they try to move into position to hit a fish with a thrown ball. A team whose fish is hit by a tossed ball immediately becomes the hunter.

Scoring: Teams are penalized 1 point for each time their fish are hit with a thrown ball. The team conceding the fewest points wins the competition.

Practice tips: This game requires a fairly high level of skill, because players must pass and receive the ball while moving at gamelike speed throughout the area. It is not appropriate for novice players or players who cannot demonstrate adequate passing and receiving skills.

CHAPTER 3

Dribbling, Shielding, and Tackling Games

Dribbling in soccer serves much the same function as dribbling in basketball—it enables a player to maintain possession of the ball while running past opponents. Effective dribbling skills used in appropriate situations can break down a defense and are vital to a team's attack. On the flip side, excessive dribbling in inappropriate areas of the field or in inopportune situations will disrupt the team play required for creating good scoring opportunities. Players must be taught to recognize situations where dribbling skills can be used to best advantage and then to respond accordingly. In general, dribbling skills can be used most effectively in the attacking third of the field nearest the opponent's goal. A player who can take on (dribble past) an opponent in that area has created a potential scoring opportunity—or at least a situation that can lead to a scoring opportunity. Dribbling should be limited in the middle and defending thirds of the field, areas where the potential penalty (i.e., a goal against) for possession loss is greater than the potential reward of beating an opponent on the dribble.

Two general dribbling styles are typically observed in game situations. Players use short, choppy steps and sudden changes of speed and direction when dribbling in tight spaces, areas where opponents are challenging for the ball. They keep the ball close to their feet at all times. In such situations, eluding defenders and protecting the ball are of paramount importance.

Conversely, when players dribble the ball in open space, ball protection is less important than moving with the ball at speed. To run with the ball at speed, players push the ball ahead several strides, usually with the outside surface of the instep, then sprint to the ball push it again.

Unlike many other soccer skills, there is no single correct technique used to dribble the ball. For this reason, dribbling is often referred to as an art rather than a skill. Players should develop their own dribbling style as long as it achieves the primary objectives of beating an opponent while maintaining possession of the ball. Granted, key elements such as deceptive body feints, sudden changes of speed and direction, and close control of the ball are common to all successful dribbling styles. The ways in which players incorporate such maneuvers into their own dribbling style can vary, however. In essence, if a dribbling style works for a player, then it is appropriate for the player.

Shielding skills are often used in conjunction with dribbling skills to protect the ball from an opponent challenging for possession. To shield the ball, the player positions his body between the ball and the opponent who is attempting to steal it. The ball is controlled with the foot farthest from the opponent, and the dribbler must readjust his position in response to pressure from the opponent. This technique is also referred to as screening the ball.

Tackling is strictly a defensive skill used to steal the ball from an opponent. Three different techniques—the block tackle, poke tackle, and slide tackle—are used, depending on the situation. The block tackle is used when an opponent is dribbling directly at a defender. The poke and slide tackles are used when a defender is approaching the dribbler from the side or from behind. The block tackle has advantages over the poke and slide tackles. The block allows for greater body control and enables the defender to initiate an immediate counterattack once the ball has been won. In addition, if the player fails to win the ball, he is still in position to recover and chase after the opponent.

The practice games in this section emphasize the development of dribbling, shielding, and tackling skills, often within the same game. Most exercises also involve a degree of fitness training because players are moving continuously throughout the games.

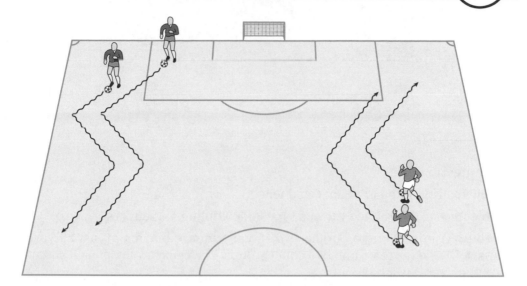

Minutes: 5 to 10

Players: Unlimited (in pairs)

Objective: To improve dribbling ability through the use of subtle body feints, sudden changes of speed and direction, and deceptive foot movements

Setup: Pair each player with a partner. Play on half of a regulation field, one ball per player.

Procedure: Partners dribble randomly throughout the area, one leading while the other closely follows. The trailing player attempts to mimic, or shadow, the movements of the leader. Partners change positions every 45 to 60 seconds on your command.

Scoring: None

Practice tips: Encourage players to keep their heads up as much as possible while dribbling to maximize their field of vision. Emphasize fluid and controlled movement with the ball. You can make the exercise more challenging by requiring players to increase their dribbling speed or by reducing the playing area so that players must keep close control of the ball within a confined space.

Minutes: 5 to 10

Players: Unlimited (2 equal-sized teams)

Objectives: To practice various types of dribbling maneuvers

Setup: Use markers to outline two 15-yard-square playing areas, 20 yards apart. Divide the team into two equal groups. Place one group in each square; each player has a ball.

Procedure: All the players from each group dribble within their square, using all surfaces of the foot to control the ball. On your signals, players change direction, change speeds, and practice deceptive foot movements, such as step-overs, within their square. On the command "Go," players from each group dribble at top speed from their square into the opponent's square. Once in the square, players continue to dribble among themselves until you signal them to return to their original grid. Repeat several times.

Scoring: The group whose players all get into the opponent's square first is awarded 1 point. The first team to total 5 points wins the game.

Practice tips: To make the game more difficult, reduce the size of the squares and increase the distance between squares.

Minutes: 5

Players: Unlimited (2 equal-sized teams)

Objectives: To practice dribbling maneuvers, changes of direction and speed, deceptive body feints

Setup: Use markers to outline a 30-yard-square playing area. Divide the group into two equal teams. To begin, designate one team as the hounds—those players are spaced randomly throughout the area and are stationary. Designate the other team as the dogcatchers. The dogcatchers each begin with a ball.

Procedure: The dogcatchers dribble randomly throughout the area, moving among the hounds while rehearsing changes of speed, direction, and deceptive dribbling maneuvers. After 45 to 60 seconds of continuous dribbling, give the command of "Release the hounds." On that signal each dogcatcher tags the nearest hound and turns her into a dogcatcher. The new dogcatcher begins to dribble, and the former dogcatcher becomes a hound and assumes a stationary position. Continue for several rounds, with groups alternating between dogcatchers and hounds.

Scoring: None

Practice tips: Increase the size of the area to increase the physical demands of the game.

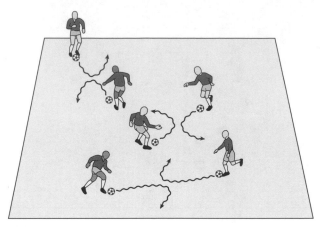

Minutes: 5 to 10

Players: Unlimited

Objectives: To practice dribbling skills; to incorporate changes of direction and speed into dribbling maneuvers

Setup: Use markers to outline a 25-yard-square playing area. All players start within the area, each with a ball.

Procedure: On your command, players begin dribbling randomly within the area, maintaining close control of the ball at all times. Players should consider themselves magnets with similar charges—they repel one another. Any time a dribbler comes near another dribbler, he immediately changes course and moves in a different direction.

Scoring: None

Practice tips: Encourage players to use sudden changes of direction and speed as they are repelled by players, all the while maintaining close control of the ball.

Minutes: 60-second rounds with short rests in between rounds (8 to 10 rounds)

Players: Unlimited

Objectives: To develop the ability to suddenly change speed and direction while dribbling; to practice stopping and restarting the ball quickly

Setup: Designate a 25-yard-square playing area. Each player has a ball.

Procedure: On your command, all players dribble among themselves. On the command of "Green light," they speed up their dribble and move as quickly as possible within the area without losing control of their ball. On the command of "Yellow light," they slow their dribble but continue to move. On the command of "Red light," they stop their ball using the sole of the foot to pin it to the ground. Issue commands in random order for a period of 60 seconds, rest for 15 seconds, and then repeat.

Scoring: None

Practice tips: Players should keep close control of the ball at all times while maintaining balance and body control. You can vary the frequency of commands so that players cannot anticipate your sequence. This game is most appropriate for younger players who are learning the basic components of effective dribbling skills.

Minutes: 5 to 10

Players: Unlimited

Objectives: To practice dribbling in a confined area; to alleviate defensive pressure through sudden changes of speed and direction

Setup: Use markers to outline a 30-yard-square playing area. Designate two players as defenders who stand outside of the area. All other players, each with a ball, start within the square. Each player tucks a colored scrimmage vest into the back of her shorts so that it hangs out.

Procedure: All players within the square begin dribbling in random fashion. On your command, the defenders sprint into the area to chase the dribblers and pull the scrimmage vests from their shorts. Dribblers use sudden changes of speed, direction, or both to evade the defenders. If a dribbler's vest is pulled out, she immediately becomes a defender and attempts to steal another dribbler's vest. A defender who captures a vest tucks it into her shorts, takes possession of the dribbler's ball, and becomes a dribbler. A dribbler must maintain possession of her ball at all times; she is not permitted to leave it in an effort to evade the defenders.

Scoring: None

Practice tips: Encourage dribblers to keep their head up as much as possible in order to be aware of the movements of the defenders.

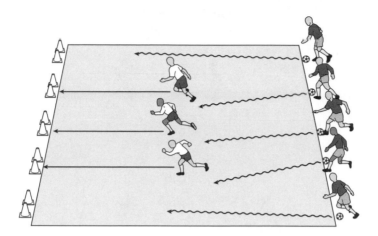

Minutes: 10

Players: 8 to 16

Objectives: To practice dribbling at speed, with head up and vision on the field

Setup: Use markers to outline a 30-yard-square playing area. Position three players in the center of the field area, facing one of the sidelines. Station the remaining players, each with a ball, on the sideline facing the middle players. Use cones or plastic discs to make a series of minigoals, 2 yards wide, on the opposite sideline. There should be as many minigoals as there are players on the opposite sideline with a ball.

Procedure: On the coach's command, the three middle players, who are without balls, sprint back to the sideline behind them; each takes a position in one of the minigoals to block the entrance. At the same instant the players on the opposite sideline, each with a ball, dribble as fast as they can across the square and through an open goal. Once a dribbler goes through an open goal, that goal is considered closed to any other dribbler. The three dribblers who fail to get through an open goal serve as the middle players for the next round.

Scoring: Award a dribbler 1 point if he dribbles through an open goal. After a series of rounds, the player totaling the most points wins the game.

Practice tips: You can vary the exercise by instructing the middle players, without balls, to actually try to win a ball by tackling or knocking it out of the area.

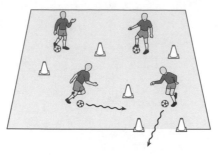

Minutes: 5 to 10

Players: Unlimited

Objectives: To practice dribbling at varying speeds where space is limited

Setup: Use markers to outline two 15-yard-square playing areas, about 10 yards apart. Set a number of discs or cones at various spots within each field to serve as obstacles to dribbling. Also set up a 4-yard-wide goal at the corner of each field, on the sideline nearest to the other field. Position the goals diagonally opposite one another. Split the team into two groups and have one group in each field. Each player requires a ball.

Procedure: All players begin dribbling within their field, avoiding the obstacles and other players. On the coach's commands of "First gear," "Second gear," or "Third gear," the players speed up or slow down their dribbling speed, all the while keeping the balls close to their feet. On the command of "Switch fields," all players dribble out of their field through the corner goal and into the opposite field through the corner goal of that field. When switching fields, the dribblers must keep their heads up to avoid colliding with players from the other field who are also switching fields. Play continuously for 10 minutes or so, with players constantly changing speeds and switching from one field to the other.

Scoring: None

Practice tips: This game is most appropriate for young players who are learning the subtleties of various dribbling techniques.

 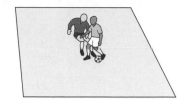

Minutes: 30-second rounds (play a series of rounds)

Players: Unlimited (in pairs, one ball per pair)

Objectives: To develop dribbling and shielding skills, to practice the poke tackle technique; to enhance fitness

Setup: Each pair marks off a 10-yard-square playing area. One player, with a ball, stands within the square. Her partner is outside the square to begin.

Procedure: The player without the ball (defender) enters the field area and tries to poke the ball away from the dribbler, who attempts to shield the ball from the defender by proper positioning of the body in relation to the ball and defender. The dribbler should use sudden changes of speed, direction, or both to elude the tackle. Play for a 30-second round, after which players switch roles and repeat. Play a number of rounds.

Scoring: Assess 1 penalty point to the dribbler for each time her ball is poked out of the field area. The player totaling the fewest penalty points after a series of rounds wins the competition.

Practice tips: Enlarge the field area for younger players to provide more space in which to elude the defender. Lengthen the rounds to 45 seconds or more for older, more accomplished players.

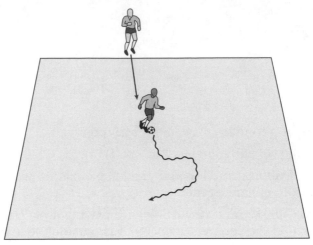

Minutes: 60-second intervals

Players: Unlimited (in pairs, one ball per pair)

Objectives: To develop the ability to dribble away from pressure

Setup: Play within a 25-yard square field area.

Procedure: The player with the ball dribbles within the area; his partner waits for the coach's command to enter the area and attempt to tag the dribbler. After each tag, the dribbler should quickly change direction and speed to create distance from the chaser. Continue for 60 seconds at maximum effort. Players then switch roles and repeat. Play several 60 second rounds.

Scoring: The dribbler is assessed 1 penalty point for each tag. The player with the fewer penalty points in 60 seconds wins the round. The player winning the most rounds wins the game.

Practice tips: Dribbler must keep the ball within range of control when attempting to elude the chaser.

Minutes: 12

Players: Unlimited (groups of 3)

Objective: To improve dribbling and shielding skills; to improve the ability to recognize and avoid defensive pressure

Setup: Use markers to outline a 15- by 20-yard playing area for each group. Three players, each with a ball, stand on the perimeter of the area. Designate one player as It; the others are chasers.

Procedure: The player who is It dribbles into the area. The chasers, who are also dribbling, attempt to follow closely. Once in position, chasers try to pass and contact It's ball with their own. It attempts to elude the chasers through sudden changes of speed and direction while maintaining close control of the ball. Play for 60 seconds, after which players switch roles and repeat the game. Continue until each player has taken three turns being It.

Scoring: The It player is assessed 1 penalty point each time her ball is contacted by one of the chaser's balls. The player with the fewest penalty points at the end of the game wins.

Practice tips: Make the game more challenging by adding an additional chaser to the game or reducing the size of the playing area.

36 First to the Cone ⚽⚽

Minutes: 12 (in 60-second periods)

Players: Unlimited (in pairs, one ball per pair)

Objectives: To rehearse the use of deceptive foot movements and body feints to unbalance an opponent; to practice sudden changes of speed and direction; to improve mobility and agility with and without the ball; to develop aerobic endurance

Setup: For each pair of players place two cones or markers 12 yards apart on the sideline or end line of the field. Partners face one another on opposite sides of the line, midway between the markers. One player, the attacker, has the ball while the other plays as the defender.

Procedure: The attacker attempts to dribble laterally to either marker before the defender can get positioned there. Neither player may cross the line that separates them. Play continuously for 90 seconds. After a short rest, players exchange possession of the ball and repeat. Play six rounds.

Scoring: The attacker scores 1 point each time he beats the defender to a marker with the ball under control. The player who scores the most points wins the game.

Practice tips: Encourage the attacker to combine deceptive body movements with sudden changes of speed and direction to unbalance the defender. Defenders must maintain balance and body control at all times. To make the game more physically demanding, increase the distance between the cones to 15 yards. As a variation, organize a tournament in which winners advance to play different opponents.

Minutes: 10

Players: Unlimited (in pairs, one ball per pair)

Objectives: To improve dribbling speed; to develop aerobic endurance; to generate a competitive training atmosphere

Setup: Play on a regulation field. Use the front edge of one penalty area as the starting line and the halfway line as the turnaround line. Each player teams up with a partner and stands along the starting line. One ball required for each pair.

Procedure: On the command of "Go!" one member of each pair dribbles at maximum speed to the halfway line, turns, and dribbles back to the start line. She then gives possession of the ball to her partner, who in turn dribbles the circuit at top speed.

Scoring: The first pair to complete the circuit (penalty area to the halfway line and back to penalty area) wins the race. Run at least 10 races, with short rests between each.

Practice tips: The technique used when dribbling at speed differs from that used when dribbling for close control in tight spaces. Rather than using short, choppy steps while keeping the ball close to their feet, players use longer strides as they push the ball two or three yards ahead and sprint to it before pushing it again. Adjust the race distance to accommodate the ages and abilities of your players. Shorten the distance for players 10 years old and under.

38 Slalom Dribbling Relay ⚽⚽

Minutes: 10 to 15

Players: Unlimited (equal-sized teams of 3 to 5 players)

Objectives: To enhance dribbling speed with close control of the ball; to improve fitness

Setup: Teammates line up in single file facing a line of five to eight markers spaced three yards apart. The first player in each line has possession of a ball.

Procedure: On the command "Go!" the first player in each line dribbles the length of the slalom course as quickly as possible, weaving in and out of the markers first to last and then reversing the weave back to the start line. On returning to the starting line, the dribbler exchanges the ball with the next player in line, who repeats the slalom circuit. Teammates dribble the course in turn until all players have completed the slalom. The team whose players complete the course in the shortest time wins the race. Repeat the race several times.

Scoring: Award 10 team points for winning a race, 8 points for second place, and 6 points for third place. Deduct 1 team point for each marker bypassed or knocked over. Determine point totals by subtracting the total number of penalty points from points awarded for the team's order of finish in the race. The first team to 40 points wins the event.

Practice tips: To make the game more difficult, reduce the distance between markers or increase the number of markers.

Minutes: 10 to 15

Players: Unlimited (2 equal-sized teams)

Objectives: To improve dribbling speed and control; to develop individual defending skills

Setup: Use markers to outline a 40-yard-square playing area. The size of the area may vary depending on the number of players involved. Mark off a 5-yard-square safety zone in each corner of the field area. Organize two teams of equal numbers, assigning a name to each team (such as Blues and Reds). Use colored vests to differentiate teams. All players begin within the area, each with a ball.

Procedure: At your command, players of both teams dribble randomly within the area while avoiding the safety zones. After 10 to 15 seconds, shout out one of the team names. At this point all members of that team attempt to dribble into a safety zone, but with one restriction: They can't dribble into the safety zone closest to them. The other team's players, the wolves, immediately leave their balls and attempt to tag (with a hand) the opposing players, the sheep, before the sheep reach a safety zone. Sheep are safe once they enter a safety zone. The round ends when all of the sheep have been tagged or have dribbled into a safety zone. At this point, players from both teams return to the center of the area and restart the game for round 2. Play several rounds, with teams alternating as wolves and sheep.

Scoring: Sheep who reach a safety zone without being tagged score 1 team point. The team scoring the most points after several repetitions of the game wins the competition.

Practice tips: For advanced players, enlarge the playing area or require wolves to dribble a ball while giving chase.

40 Tackle All Balls ⚽⚽

Minutes: 10

Players: Unlimited

Objectives: To practice the block and poke tackle techniques; to develop dribbling and shielding skills; to improve fitness

Setup: Use markers to form a rectangular area about 25 by 35 yards. Designate two or three players as defenders, who stand, without balls, outside the playing area. The remaining players, each with a ball, stand inside the area.

Procedure: Play begins with the inside players (attackers) dribbling randomly within the area. On your command, defenders enter the area to give chase and gain possession of a ball. Defenders use the block or poke tackle techniques to steal the attackers' balls. A player who loses his ball to a defender immediately becomes a defender and attempts to steal someone else's ball. A defender gaining possession of a ball becomes an attacker. Play is continuous as players alternate playing as defenders and attackers.

Scoring: None

Practice tips: Prohibit slide tackles because of the crowded conditions. In order to make the game more challenging for the dribblers, you can decrease the area size or designate additional defenders.

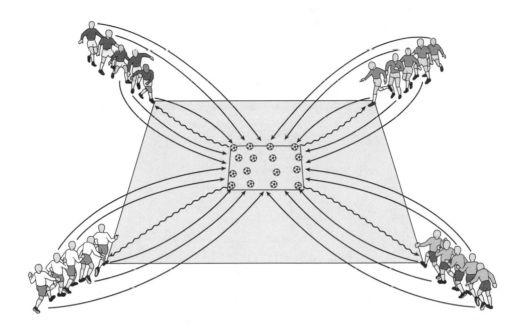

Minutes: 10 to 15

Players: 20 to 24 (4 equal-sized teams)

Objectives: To improve dribbling speed; to practice the block and poke tackle techniques; to practice defensive recovery runs; to develop aerobic endurance

Setup: Use markers to outline a 50-yard square. Outline a 10-yard square in the center of the larger area. Organize four equal teams and have one team in each corner of the larger square. Place a supply of balls, four fewer balls than the number of players involved, in the small central square. Use colored vests to differentiate teams.

Procedure: On the command of "Go!" players from all four teams sprint to the middle, compete for possession of a ball, and attempt to dribble the ball back to their original corner. Because there are fewer balls than players, the players who do not immediately secure a ball must chase after opponents and prevent them from returning balls to their corner by tackling their ball. The round ends when all the balls have been returned to the corners. Reposition all balls in the center square and repeat the activity. Play at least 10 rounds.

Scoring: The group that returns the most balls to their corner is awarded 1 point. A ball must be dribbled under control and stopped in the corner to count as a point scored. The team scoring the most points after 10 rounds wins.

Practice tips: Prohibit slide tackles, particularly those initiated from behind.

42 **Knockout** ⚽ ⚽

Minutes: 10 to 15

Players: 10 to 20

Objectives: To develop dribbling, shielding, and tackling skills; to improve fitness

Setup: Use markers to outline a rectangular area about 25 by 30 yards. All players start within the playing area, each with a ball.

Procedure: To begin, players dribble randomly within the area, avoiding all other players and keeping the ball within close control of their feet. On a signal from you, the exercise becomes "Knockout." Each player attempts to kick other players' balls out of the area while maintaining possession of his own ball. A player whose ball is kicked out of the area leaves the game, retrieves her ball, and practices juggling the ball at the side of the field area until the game concludes. The game ends when only one player remains in possession of her ball. Repeat the activity several times.

Scoring: The last player with possession of the ball wins the game.

Practice tips: Vary the size of the area depending on the number of players. Require players to use either the block or poke tackle when attempting to steal a teammate's ball. Prohibit slide tackles because of the crowded conditions.

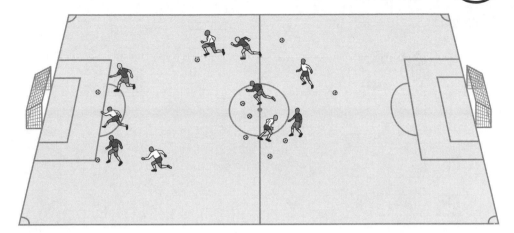

Minutes: 10 to 15

Players: 10 to 20 (2 equal-sized teams of 5 to 10)

Objectives: To improve dribbling speed; to develop general endurance; to practice recovery runs and tackling skills

Setup: Play on a regulation field. Organize two teams of equal numbers and give each a name, for instance, Strikers and Kickers. Players from both teams, each with a ball, stand in the center circle of the field. Each team defends an end line of the field. Use colored vests to differentiate teams. No goals or goalkeepers are necessary.

Procedure: To begin, players from both teams dribble randomly within the center circle. After several seconds of continuous dribbling, you shout out a team name, such as "Strikers!" On that command, all Striker players leave the circle to dribble at top speed toward the Kickers' end line. Kickers immediately leave their balls to give chase, attempting to catch and dispossess Striker players before they can dribble their balls over the Kicker's end line. A Kicker who steals a ball attempts to return it into the center circle by dribbling. The round ends when all balls have been dribbled over the end line or returned into the center circle. Play 8 to 10 rounds, alternating teams from attacking to defending.

Scoring: The attacking team scores 1 point for each ball dribbled over the opponent's end line. The defending team scores 2 points for each ball stolen and dribbled back to the center circle. The team scoring the most points wins the round, and the team winning the most total rounds wins the game.

Practice tips: Adjust the field size to accommodate the ages and abilities of your players. Younger players (12 and under) should use a three-quarter field. Defending players should take the most direct recovery run to a point between the end line and the opponent they are tracking down. Once they are goal side, defenders can challenge for the ball. Prohibit the use of slide tackles from behind.

44 Rob the Bank ⚽⚽

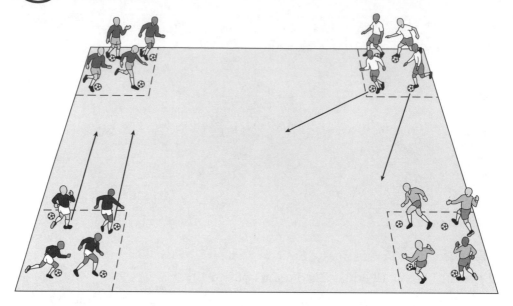

Minutes: 10 to 15

Players: Unlimited (4 equal-sized teams)

Objectives: To develop dribbling and tackling skills; to improve fitness; to create a competitive and enjoyable training atmosphere

Setup: Use markers to outline a 50-yard-square playing area. Mark a 10-yard square in each corner of the larger square. Divide the group into four teams. Place one team in each corner square; that square is considered the team's bank. One ball is required for each player.

Procedure: Each team deposits all of its balls in its own bank. One player on each team is designated as the bank guard whose responsibility is to protect the team's balls from opponents trying to steal them. All other players on the team are snatchers who search for and attempt to snatch balls from other teams' banks and deposit them in their own bank. On your command, the game begins. Snatchers run to other banks and try to steal the balls deposited there and deposit them in their own banks. The bank guard attempts to protect her team's bank by tackling the ball from a snatcher attempting to steal it.

Scoring: The team with the most balls in the bank after 2 minutes is awarded 1 point. Play several rounds. The first team to score 3 points wins the game.

Practice tips: Designate two bank guards for each team to make the game more difficult for the snatchers.

Minutes: 10 to 15

Players: Unlimited

Objectives: To practice dribbling and tackling skills in the same activity; to encourage competition within the team

Setup: Use markers to outline a 40-yard-square area. Mark a smaller 15-yard square in the center of the larger square. Divide the group into two teams of equal numbers. One team starts within the smaller square, each player with a ball. The other team's players begin in the area outside of the small central square, without balls.

Procedure: Players within the smaller square dribble at random among themselves. Players on the opposing team jog at random in the area outside of the smaller square. On your command, players with a ball dribble out of the small square and attempt to dribble out of the field area. The opponents try to prevent dribblers from reaching the perimeter by tackling the ball and kicking it away. A dribbler who dribbles out of the area is awarded 1 point. Players on each team tally points for the team score. Teams then switch roles and repeat.

Scoring: Players on each team add up individual scores to get the team score. The team scoring the most points after six rounds wins the competition.

Practice tips: Prohibit the use of slide tackles to win the ball; players should use block and poke tackles only.

Minutes: 10

Players: Unlimited (in pairs, one ball per pair)

Objectives: To develop the ability to dribble at and beat a defender; to practice the block and poke tackle techniques

Setup: Pair players with a partner for competition. Outline a playing area 20 yards long by 10 yards wide for each pair. Pairs stand across from one another on opposing end lines to begin; one has the ball.

Procedure: The player with the ball serves it to her partner and immediately sprints forward to defend her end line, which represents her partner's goal. The player receiving the ball attempts to dribble past the defender to the end line. Play continues until the dribbler crosses the end line, the defender wins the ball, or the ball leaves the field area; whichever occurs first. Players then switch roles and repeat. Play a total of 20 rounds, with players alternating roles each round.

Scoring: The dribbler is awarded 1 point for each time she beats the defender on the dribble to the end line

Practice tips: Widen the playing area for younger players to create a wider channel in which they can attempt to beat the opponent.

CHAPTER 4

Passing and Receiving Games

Passing and receiving skills provide the vital thread that connects the individual parts of the team, the players, into a smoothly functioning whole that is greater than the sum of its parts. The ability of players to pass the ball accurately and with the proper pace is necessary for creating successful attacking combinations. The velocity of the pass should not be too hard or too easy—the ball should be played firmly to the feet of a teammate, but not so hard that the pass will be difficult to control. Equally important is the ability to skillfully receive and control balls arriving on the ground and through the air. All players, including the goalkeeper, should become confident and competent in passing and receiving the ball.

Passes should be played along the ground rather than through the air when possible. Ground passes are easier to control and can usually be played with greater accuracy than lofted passes. There will be times during the match, however, when the situation dictates that the ball should be played through the air. For example, an opponent may be blocking the passing lane between the player on the ball and a teammate who is stationed in a dangerous attacking position. Or a player might decide to flight the ball into the open space behind the opponent's defense for a teammate to run onto. In such situations the pass can be lofted (chipped) through the air. Three surfaces of the foot—the inside of the instep, the outside of the instep, and the full instep (laces of the shoe)—are used to pass the ball along the ground. The full instep surface of the foot is also used to flight the ball over distance.

Rolling balls are generally received and controlled with either the inside or outside surface of the foot, although the sole of the foot can also be used to control an oncoming ball. Balls taken directly out of the air can be received with the instep, thigh, chest, or, in rare instances, the head. In all cases, the player should slightly withdraw the receiving surface as the ball arrives to cushion the impact and provide a soft target. A player's first touch on the ball as it arrives is the most important touch. Players who can recognize pressure and control the ball into the space away from a challenging opponent, rather than stopping the ball completely, afford themselves additional time and space in which to initiate their next movement. Proper positioning of the body as the ball arrives is also important for maintaining possession, particularly when an opponent is challenging to win the ball. Emphasize these points in all passing and receiving exercises.

The games in this section focus on the development of fundamental passing and receiving skills, although in many of the exercises, other soccer skills are included as well. The overriding objective of each game is for players to become more competent and confident in their passing and receiving skills in gamelike situations. You can modify the games to emphasize specific passing and receiving skills. Most can be easily adapted to accommodate the age, ability, and physical maturity of your players.

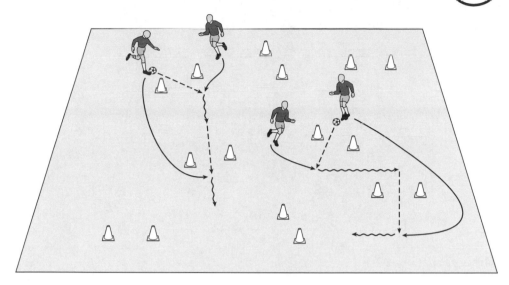

Minutes: 5

Players: Unlimited (in pairs, 1 ball per pair)

Objectives: To practice passing and receiving the ball with a teammate while moving throughout a field space

Setup: Outline a field area of 50 yards square. Use markers to designate 8 to 12 small goals (2 yards wide) placed randomly throughout the field. Organize players into pairs, with one ball per pair.

Procedure: Partners move throughout the field area, playing combinations and passing through the goals to one another as often as possible. Partners are not permitted to pass through the same goal twice in succession. After completing a pass through a goal, the receiving player dribbles off toward a different goal while her partner sprints forward to receive a return pass directed through a minigoal.

Scoring: Each pair of partners competes with the other pairs. The pair that completes the greatest number of passes through the minigoals wins the competition.

Practice tips: Emphasize accuracy and correct pacing of passes. To increase the pressure on the passers, add a chasing defender to the exercise.

(48) Connect the Dots ⚽

Minutes: 10

Players: Unlimited (in groups of 5 to 8)

Objectives: To develop passing and receiving skills when moving throughout a field area; to improve endurance

Setup: Use markers to outline a 30-yard by 40-yard playing area for each group. Players begin within this area. Assign each player in a group a number beginning with 1 and continuing through the number of players in the group. Two players in each group have a ball to begin.

Procedure: All players begin moving within their group area. Each group will work on completing a circuit by passing the ball from a lower numbered player to the next numbered player. For example: player 1 always passes to player 2, player 2 to 3, and so on. The highest numbered player in the group passes to player 1 to complete the circuit and connect all of the dots. Begin the play by having those players with a ball dribble; those without a ball continually reposition to make themselves available to receive a pass from the player numbered below him. All players are expected to move continuously during the exercise as they pass to the teammate numbered above them and receive passes from the teammate numbered below them.

Scoring: None

Practice tips: The game should flow continuously as players dribble, pass, and receive the ball. Encourage players not to stop the ball completely as they receive it; rather, they should receive and control the ball in the direction (space) of their next movement. Make the game more challenging by placing restrictions on players (such as having them pass with only their weakest foot or with only the outside or instep surface of the foot).

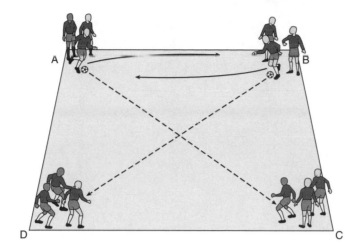

Minutes: 5

Players: 12 to 16 (4 equal-sized groups)

Objectives: To develop the ability to prepare and pass the ball accurately using only two touches to control and play the ball; to incorporate fitness training into a technical session

Setup: Use markers to outline a 12-yard square. Three or four players line up at each corner (A, B, C, and D) of the square. Corner A is diagonally across from C, and B is diagonally across the square from D. The first players at corners A and B begin with a ball.

Procedure: The first players in line at corners A and B pass the ball diagonally across the square to corners C and D, respectively, and then switch corners, sprinting along the side of the square as passer A goes to the end of the line at corner B and passer B goes to the end of the line at corner A. At the same time, the first players at corners C and D receive and prepare the ball with their first touch, return it to corners A and B with their second touch, and then switch corners. Continue the game as players pass diagonally across the square and then sprint laterally to the opposite corner.

Scoring: None

Practice tips: Vary the running and passing patterns. For example, have players pass diagonally across the square and then follow the pass to that corner, or have players pass laterally to an adjacent corner player and then sprint diagonally across the square. Emphasize the importance of passing and then moving to another area.

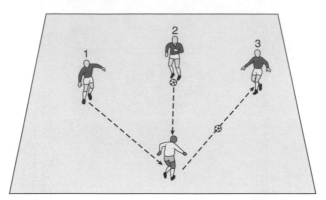

Minutes: 8 to 16

Players: Unlimited (groups of 4: 3 servers and 1 target)

Objective: To play quick, accurate one-touch ground passes to an open player while maintaining proper body shape and balance

Setup: Three players (servers) stand side by side two yards apart. The fourth player (target) faces the servers at a distance of seven yards. Servers 1 and 2 each have a ball at their feet; server 3 does not have a ball to begin.

Procedure: Server 1 begins by passing the ball to the target, who sends it using a first-time (one-touch) inside-of-the-foot pass to server 3. Server 2 immediately plays a ball to the target, who returns it to server 1, who is without a ball. Server 3 sends the ball (received from the target) back to the target, who sends it to server 2, and the cycle repeats. Continue the game at maximum speed, and the target player returns each pass to the server who is without a ball. After 2 minutes of continuous passing, one of the servers switches position with the target player. Repeat until each player has taken a turn as the target player.

Scoring: Perform as many passes as possible without errors in 2 minutes.

Practice tips: Passes from servers to target must be accurate and properly weighted. The target player must play all passes first-time, and must keep the head up in order to know which server is without a ball. If a ball goes astray, the game continues with the second ball, with no stop in play.

Variations: The target player can pass the ball with the inside of the foot or the outside of the foot. Servers can pass the ball along the ground or use their hands to toss air balls to the target player, who must receive, control, and return the ball. Advanced players can perform this exercise while moving throughout a larger playing area.

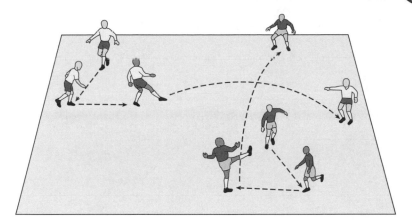

Minutes: 10

Players: Unlimited (in groups of 4 or 5)

Objectives: To develop short-, medium-, and long-range passing skills; to introduce the concept of changing the tempo of attack; to encourage players to suddenly change the point of attack

Setup: Organize players into groups of four, with one ball per group. Play in an area at least 30 by 50 yards. All groups begin within the area.

Procedure: Teammates pass to one another within their group while moving throughout the entire area. Teammates must execute passes in a short-short-long passing sequence by making two consecutive short passes (5 to 10 yards) followed by a longer pass (25 to 30 yards) designed to change the point of attack. Play continues with players using the short-short-long sequence. The short-range passes should be played on the ground; the longer pass can be played on the ground or lofted through the air.

Scoring: None; players are encouraged to repeat the short-short-long passing sequence as many times as possible in the time allotted.

Practice tips: Emphasize passing accuracy and proper pace. Perform the drill at game speed, even though there are no defenders applying pressure. Players off (without) the ball must make intelligent supporting runs to make themselves available to receive a pass in the appropriate short-short-long passing sequence. Make the game more demanding by placing restrictions on players (such as limiting the number of touches allowed) or by adding the pressure of a defending opponent(s).

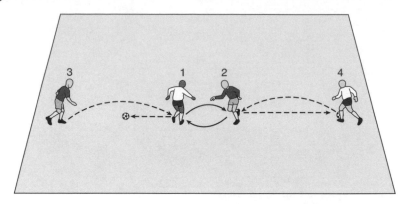

Minutes: 16 minutes (8 segments of 2 minutes each)

Players: Unlimited (in groups of 4)

Objectives: To execute accurate one-touch passes; to develop precise checking runs; to improve fitness

Setup: Players 1 and 2 stand back to back midway between players 3 and 4 (servers), who are stationed 15 yards apart; each server with a ball.

Procedure: The exercise begins with players 1 and 2 checking (moving toward) the server they are facing. Servers 3 and 4 make a firm pass to the checking players, 1 and 2, who return (bump) the ball to the servers with a one-touch pass. After bumping the ball, players 1 and 2 immediately spin away and check toward the opposite server, repeating the exercise. Continue at maximum speed and effort for 2 minutes, after which the checkers and servers switch roles and repeat. All one-touch bump passes are made with the inside or outside surface of the foot. Each player takes a total of four turns as a checking player.

Scoring: Players execute as many one-touch bump passes as they can in 2 minutes. The player performing the greatest number of bump passes (total of 4 rounds each) without error wins the competition.

Practice tips: Vary the type of pass used by the checking player (one-touch, two-touch, outside of the foot, and so on). Emphasize hard-checking runs toward the server and firm, crisp return passes.

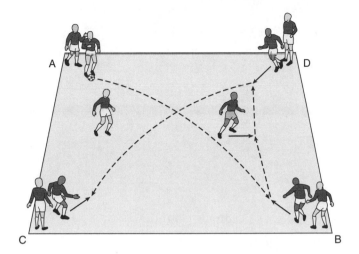

Minutes: 10

Players: 10

Objectives: To improve the ability to play flighted balls over distance with accuracy and proper pace; to practice receiving balls out of the air

Setup: Mark off a 30-yard square. Have two players at each corner (A, B, C, and D) of the square and two players (E and F) in the center of the square. Corner B is diagonally across the square from A, and corner D is diagonally across from C. Player A begins with the ball. Player F faces Corner B and E faces corner C to begin the game.

Procedure: A player in corner A serves a lofted pass diagonally across the square to a player in corner B. Player B lays the ball off to middle player F, who turns the ball and plays to corner player D. D serves a lofted pass diagonally across the square to a player at corner C. C lays the ball off to middle player E, who turns and plays to the next player in line at corner A. Repeat the pattern and have players switch positions in the square by following their pass and lining up at the corner they passed to.

Scoring: Award a player 1 point for each ball he flights diagonally across the square that can be received directly out of the air by the receiving player. The player totaling the most points after 10 minutes wins the contest.

Practice tips: Encourage players to drive their instep beneath the ball with a short, powerful kicking motion in order to generate sufficient height and distance on the flighted pass. This game may be too difficult for younger players who do not possess the skill required to perform the exercise.

Minutes: 5 to 10 minutes (1-minute rounds)

Players: Unlimited (in groups of 3)

Objectives: To juggle the ball in the air by passing and receiving with various surfaces of the body

Setup: Each group plays in its own area approximately 15 yards square.

Procedure: Players keep the ball in the air by passing and receiving the ball with various surfaces (instep, thigh, chest, head). Play for a series of 1-minute rounds.

Scoring: The group that allows the ball to drop to the ground the fewest number of times in a 60-second round wins the round. Play for a number of consecutive rounds. The group winning the most rounds wins the game.

Practice tips: As a variation: require players to move about when juggling, to receive with a specific body part, or to pass among themselves with a specific number of touches on the ball.

Minutes: 10 to 15

Minutes: 10 to 15

Players: 10 to 14 (2 equal-sized teams)

Objectives: To receive and control balls dropping out of the air using various body surfaces; to encourage proper support positioning for players in the vicinity of the ball; to improve endurance

Setup: Use markers to outline a playing area of 30 yards by 40 yards. Organize the group into two teams of equal number and have both teams begin within the area. Use colored scrimmage vests to differentiate teams. Award one team the ball to begin.

Procedure: The team with the ball plays Keep Away from its opponents but does so by tossing the ball rather than kicking it. Players must receive and control passes on their instep, thigh, chest, or head, and then catch the ball with their hands before it drops to the ground. Players may take up to four steps while in possession of the ball before passing to a teammate. The opposing (defending) team gains possession of the ball by intercepting a pass (with the hands) or when an opponent fails to control the ball before it drops to the ground. Players are not permitted to wrestle the ball away from an opponent once he has received and controlled it.

Scoring: Award 1 team point for 10 consecutive passes. The team scoring the most points wins.

Practice tips: Encourage players to provide a soft target by withdrawing the receiving surface (foot, thigh, and so on) as the ball arrives to cushion the impact. Adjust the size of the area to accommodate the number of players. This game might not be appropriate for younger players who have not mastered fundamental receiving skills.

Minutes: 3 minutes per round or until all players are eliminated, whichever comes first

Players: 12 to 20 (2 equal-sized teams)

Objectives: To improve passing and dribbling skills; to develop agility, mobility, and fitness

Setup: Use markers to outline a 35-yard-square playing area. Team A players begin within the area without soccer balls; team B players begin outside the area, each with a ball.

Procedure: At your command, team B players dribble into the area and attempt to pass their balls to make contact with team A players. All passes must be made with the inside or outside surface of the foot and must contact team A players below the knees. Team A players are free to move anywhere within the area to avoid being hit by a ball. Any player struck with a ball below the knees is eliminated from the game and leaves the playing area to practice individual ball juggling until the game is completed. Play for 3 minutes or until all team A players have been eliminated, whichever comes first. Repeat with teams reversing roles.

Scoring: The team eliminating all its opponents in the least amount of time wins; or if all players are not eliminated, the team that eliminates the greatest number of opponents wins. Repeat the game several times, switching team roles each time.

Practice tips: Encourage players to dribble as close as they can to their intended target before passing the ball. Emphasize passing accuracy rather than power. You can adjust the playing area size to accommodate the ages and abilities of your players.

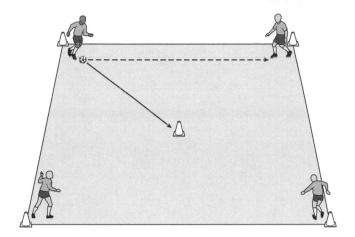

Minutes: 5 to 10 minutes

Players: Unlimited (in groups of 4)

Objectives: To pass, receive, and move to open space

Setup: Position 4 flat disc markers or cones to represent the corners of a 30-yard square. Place an additional marker near the center of the square. To begin, one player stands at each corner marker; the central marker is open. One ball required per group.

Procedure: The player with the ball passes to any of the other players and then sprints to the open marker. The player receiving the ball prepares it with her first touch, passes to another player with the second touch, and then sprints to the newly-open marker. The drill continues with players receiving, passing, and moving to the open marker.

Scoring: None

Practice tips: This drill reinforces the important concept of moving into open space after passing the ball. Players should control and prepare the ball with their first touch, and then release the pass as quickly as possible before sprinting to the open marker.

Minutes: 15 (or 10 points, whichever comes first)

Players: Unlimited (3 equal-sized teams)

Objectives: To develop passing skills; to improve general endurance

Setup: Use markers to outline a playing area 30 by 40 yards. Station the three teams in the playing area. Use colored scrimmage vests to differentiate teams. Designate one player on each team as the fox who wears a distinctive shirt or vest. Each team has possession of two soccer balls; six balls are in play at all times.

Procedure: The objective is to contact an opposing team's fox below the knees with a passed ball. Players move the ball into position to pass and hit the fox by coupling dribbling with combination passing among teammates. Foxes are free to move anywhere within the playing area to avoid getting hit with a ball.

Scoring: A pass that contacts a fox below the knees scores 1 point for the team making the pass. Each team keeps the total of its points scored. The first team to total 10 points (or the team with the highest number of points after 15 minutes) wins the game.

Practice tips: This game is appropriate for players who have mastered fundamental passing skills. Reduce the area size for younger, less skilled players.

Minutes: 18

Players: 9 or 12 (3 teams of 3 or 4)

Objectives: To develop group passing combinations; to rehearse proper support movement of teammates with the ball; to practice the defensive principles of pressure, cover, and balance

Setup: Use markers to outline a field area approximately 30 by 40 yards. Station one team within the area as the defending team. The remaining two teams (attackers) space their players evenly on the perimeter of the area. You will need one ball per game.

Procedure: Attackers attempt to keep the ball away from the outnumbered defenders. Attackers are allowed to move laterally along the four perimeter lines to support their teammates and receive passes, but they may not enter the area to receive a pass, which forces the attackers to make longer distance passes. They are also limited to three or fewer touches to receive, control, and pass the ball. The outnumbered defending players must work together to close down the space available to attackers and win the ball. When a defending player intercepts the ball, he immediately returns it to an attacker. Play continuously for 6 minutes, and then repeat the game with a different team serving as defenders. Play a total of three games; each team plays one 6-minute period as defenders.

Scoring: Award the defending team 1 point each time it gains possession or forces the attacking team to play the ball outside the playing area. The attacking teams score 2 points for 8 or more consecutive passes. The highest point total after 6 minutes wins the round.

Practice tips: Defending players must work together to pressure the ball and block passing lanes. Attacking players can counter such tactics by quickly changing the point of attack (location of the ball) to prevent defenders from closing down the space. Adjust the playing area size to accommodate the ages and abilities of your players. Reducing the area size will make it more difficult for the attacking teams to complete consecutive passes.

Minutes: 15

Players: 12 to 20 (2 equal-sized teams)

Objective: To coordinate team play through effective passing combinations, proper support movement, and purposeful off-the-ball running

Setup: Play on half a regulation field. Designate one player on each team to be the target player. Use colored scrimmage vests to differentiate teams and use an additional distinctive color of clothing to designate the target. Award one team possession of the ball.

Procedure: Teams compete against one another. Each team has two primary goals: (1) to maintain possession of the ball, and (2) to complete passes to the target player. Targets should move constantly to make themselves available for passes from teammates. Change of possession occurs when an opposing player intercepts a pass or tackles the ball, when the ball travels out of the playing area, or after a pass is completed to a target. All regular soccer rules apply except the offside rule, which is waived.

Scoring: Award 1 team point for 6 consecutive passes without loss of possession; award 2 points for a pass completed to a target player. The team scoring the most points wins.

Practice tips: Reduce the area size for highly skilled players. For variations, designate two target players for each team or impose touch restrictions (such as two-touch passes only) or both.

Minutes: 15 to 20

Players: 12 (3 teams of 4)

Objective: To execute passing skills under gamelike pressures

Setup: Play within a 40 yard by 20 yard area. Organize teams of four players each. Differentiate teams with colored scrimmage vests; designate one team as the defending team to begin. The two remaining teams combine to form an eight-player attacking team. The attacking team has the ball to begin.

Procedure: The eight-player team attempts to keep the ball away from the four-player team. Attackers are limited to two touches to receive and pass the ball. Change of possession occurs when a defending player steals the ball, when an attacker plays the ball out of the area, or when an attacker uses more than two touches to control the ball. The group of four whose error caused the loss of possession immediately becomes the defending team and tries to win the ball back; members of the original defending team become attackers. Play continues as teams alternate from attack to defense upon each loss of possession.

Scoring: 10 consecutive passes without loss of possession equals 1 team point.

Practice tips: You can make the game more or less difficult depending on the age and ability of players. For example, you could allow younger players three or four touches to control the ball, while you might restrict elite players to one-touch soccer. You can also increase the number of players to play 10v5 or 12v6, which will reduce the space and time available to players for receiving and passing the ball.

Minutes: 15

Players: 15 to 21 (2 teams of 6 to 9 plus 3 neutral players)

Objective: To develop passing combinations

Setup: Play on half a regulation field. Designate three players to be neutral, and organize the remaining players into two teams of equal number. Use colored vests to differentiate the two teams and the neutral players. You'll need at least one soccer ball, but it's better to have more. Award one team possession of the ball to begin.

Procedure: The team with the ball tries to keep it from its opponents. Neutral players always combine with the team in possession to create a three-player advantage for the attacking team. All players, including the neutral ones, are allowed three or fewer touches to pass and receive the ball. Change of possession occurs when the ball is played out of bounds, when an opponent steals the ball, or when a player takes more than three touches to receive and pass the ball. Teams reverse roles immediately upon change of possession, constantly switching from attack to defense and vice versa.

Scoring: Eight consecutive passes without a loss of possession earns 1 point. The team scoring the most points wins.

Practice tips: Emphasize the importance of receiving and preparing the ball with the first touch. Quick ball movement coupled with constantly changing the point of attack is encouraged. The team in possession should stretch the field vertically and horizontally to create greater space and more time in which to receive and pass the ball. Defending players should work together to pressure the ball and compact the available space around the ball.

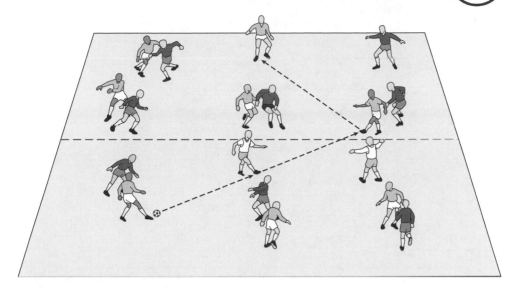

Minutes: 15 to 20

Players: 18 (2 teams of 8 plus 2 neutral players)

Objectives: To develop passing combinations to move the ball quickly and effectively to different field areas; to improve general endurance

Setup: Use markers to outline a field area of 50 yards square, divided in half by a midline. Form two teams of 8 players each; designate two additional players as neutrals who always join with the team in possession of the ball. Use colored vests to differentiate teams and the neutrals.

Procedure: The team in possession attempts to keep the ball from their opponents. All players are restricted to three or fewer touches to receive, control, and pass the ball. Teams are permitted to complete three or fewer consecutive passes in the same half of the field before switching the point of attack to the opposite half. Change of possession occurs when the ball is played out of bounds, when an opponent steals the ball, when a team makes more than three passes in a half of the field, or when a player takes more than three touches to receive and pass the ball.

Scoring: A team completing six or more consecutive passes (but no more than three consecutive passes in the same half of the field) is awarded 1 point. The team scoring the most total points wins the game.

Practice tips: Encourage players to play the ball quickly, with as few touches as possible, while constantly changing the location of the ball in response to the pressure applied by opposing players.

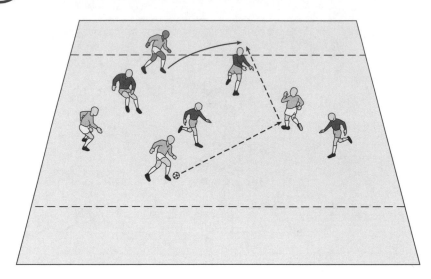

Minutes: 20

Players: 8 to 12 (2 teams of 4, 5, or 6)

Objective: To develop passing combinations used to advance the ball into dangerous attacking spaces

Setup: Use markers to outline a field area 50 yards long by 25 yards wide. Designate a zone 10 yards deep at each end, spanning the 25-yard width of the field. Start with both teams in the central area of the field between the end zones. Assign each team an end zone to defend. No goals or goalkeepers are necessary. One ball required per game.

Procedure: Play begins with a kickoff from the center of the field. Basic soccer rules apply (other than the method of scoring). The team with the ball scores 1 point by completing a pass to a player who has moved into the opponent's end zone. Defending players may not enter their own end zone to intercept passes—they must collectively position to pressure the player with the ball and block passing lanes to prevent passes from entering their end zone. Change of possession occurs when the defending team steals the ball, when the ball that goes out of play was last touched by a member of the attacking team, or after each point scored. Otherwise, play is continuous.

Scoring: The attacking team is awarded 1 point for a pass received and controlled within the opponent's end zone. The team scoring the most points wins.

Practice tips: Adjust the field size to accommodate the ages and abilities of your players. Smaller end zones make it more difficult to score points, while larger (deeper and wider) end zones make it more difficult for defending players to prevent scores. Place restrictions on players to emphasize specific aspects of play (for example, discourage excessive dribbling by limiting players to three or fewer touches of the ball before passing).

Minutes: 20

Players: 10 to 14 (2 equal-sized teams of 5 to 7)

Objectives: To develop passing and receiving skills under gamelike pressures; to develop aerobic endurance

Setup: Play between the penalty areas of a regulation field. Randomly place markers to represent five small goals (three yards wide) within the area. Use colored vests to differentiate teams. You'll need one ball. Do not use goalkeepers.

Procedure: Award one team possession of the ball to begin. Teams can score in all five goals and must defend all five goals. Players score by completing a pass through a goal to a teammate stationed on the opposite side. The ball may be passed through either side of a goal, but consecutive passes through the same goal are not allowed. Play is continuous. Change of possession occurs when the defending team steals the ball or when the ball leaving the playing area was last touched by the attacking team. Change of possession does not occur after each goal. All regular soccer rules apply except the offside rule; it is waived.

Scoring: Teams score 1 point for each pass through a goal received and controlled by a teammate. The team scoring the most points wins.

Practice tips: Prohibiting consecutive scores through the same goal encourages players to switch the point of attack to penetrate the goal area with the fewest opponents. Reduce the area size to further restrict the space and time available for players to pass and receive the ball.

Minutes: 15

Players: 20 (18 field players and 2 goalkeepers)

Objectives: To possess and advance the ball through combination passing

Setup: Outline a field area of 60 yards long by 35 yards wide with a full-sized goal on each end line. Divide the group into two teams of nine players each, plus a goalkeeper in each large goal. Teams begin behind opposite goals, facing one another. Each team designates three players as defenders and the remaining six as attackers. Place a supply of soccer balls behind each goal.

Procedure: On your command, one team attacks with six players; the opponents send their three defenders out to confront the attackers. Attacking players are limited to two touches to pass and receive the ball and must take a shot on goal within 30 seconds of initiating the attack. After a shot on goal, a goal scored, loss of possession, or the end of the 30-second time limit, the original defending team attacks with six players and their opponents defend with three players. The team scoring the most goals in 15 minutes wins the game.

Scoring: A goal scored within 30 seconds counts as 1 point.

Practice tips: Encourage the attacking team to maintain possession through combination passing and at the same time, penetrate into the opposing half as quickly as possible to create scoring opportunities. In a numbers-up situation (i.e., there are more attackers than defenders), the attacking team should take advantage of its numerical superiority and attack with speed and precision.

Minutes: 20

Players: 10 to 20 (2 equal-sized teams of 5 to 10)

Objective: To practice receiving and controlling balls dropping out of the air

Setup: Play on an outdoor volleyball or tennis court, if available. If not, use markers to form a rectangular area 20 yards wide by 40 yards long. Stretch a net or rope about 6 feet high across the center of the court. Place one team on each side of the net. You'll need one soccer ball. Award one team the serve to begin.

Procedure: Players may use their head or feet to play the ball. The server stands behind the end line. The ball must be served, from its position on the ground, over the net and land within the opponent's court to constitute a good serve. The ball may bounce once before it's returned although it's also okay to return the serve with a first-time volley. (This applies to all plays, not only service returns.) Teammates are allowed to pass to one another in the air before returning the ball over the net. A fault occurs if the serve or return fails to clear the net, the serve or return lands out of bounds, the ball bounces more than once, or a player uses arms or hands to pass or control the ball. If the serving team commits a fault, it loses the serve to opponents.

Scoring: The serving team earns 1 point for each fault committed by the receiving team. A service fault results in the loss of serve to the opponents. The first team to score 21 points wins. Play three games.

Practice tips: Soccer volleyball is a good choice for the day after a match, when players are physically fatigued and mentally drained. This game is not appropriate for younger players who lack the skill or physical maturity to serve and receive the ball out of the air.

Minutes: 10 to 15

Players: 20 to 24 (2 equal-sized teams)

Objectives: To practice passing and receiving skills under gamelike pressures of limited time, restricted space, and challenging opponents

Setup: Use markers to outline an area of 40 yards by 30 yards. Divide the group into two teams of equal numbers (teams of 10 or 12 players each). Use colored vests to differentiate teams. Divide each team into two groups of 5 or 6. Place one group of 5 or 6 players from each team within the field area; the remaining players from each team stand along the perimeter lines of the area, spaced evenly around the field. Award one team possession of the ball to begin.

Procedure: The team of 5 or 6 players with the ball within the area attempt to keep it from their opponents. Players are permitted to pass to any of their teammates, both teammates within the area and those moving along the perimeter lines. All players are limited to two or fewer touches to receive and pass the ball. Perimeter players may not move into the field to receive passes but can move laterally along the perimeter lines. The defending team gains possession when a teammate intercepts a passed ball or forces their opponents to play the ball out of the field area, or when an opposing player uses more than two touches to receive and pass the ball. Teams switch between attack and defense upon change of possession. After 3 to 4 minutes of continuous play, the players on the perimeter lines switch places with the central players, and the game continues.

Scoring: Award 1 point for eight or more consecutive passes without a loss of possession.

Practice tips: Encourage players to prepare and play the ball as quickly as possible, constantly changing the point of attack to make the opponents readjust positions. You can make the game more difficult by reducing the field space.

CHAPTER 5

Shooting and Finishing Games

During the 2006 World Cup tournament, players such as Miroslav Klose of Germany, Thierry Henry of France, Wayne Rooney of England, and Hernan Crespo of Argentina received most of the media attention—and rightly so. These players and a handful of others make up an elite group of world-class goal scorers. They are the ultimate marksmen of international soccer, players who can determine the outcome of a match with one spectacular finish. Although a goal scored is most often the result of a team effort, the player who can consistently finish the attack by putting the ball in the back of the net is a rare and valuable team member.

Scoring goals remains the single most difficult task in soccer, particularly at the higher levels of competition where team defenses are highly organized, and goalkeepers are athletic and acrobatic. Success as a goal scorer depends on several factors, one of which is the ability to shoot powerfully and accurately with either foot. Several shooting techniques are used depending on whether the ball is rolling, bouncing, or taken directly out of the air. The instep drive is used to strike a rolling or stationary ball. The full volley, half volley, and side volley are typically used to strike a bouncing ball or a ball that's dropping from above. Less tangible qualities such as determination, anticipation, confidence, composure under pressure, and a desire to score also factor into the equation.

Great goal scorers have a rare and special gift—the ability to consistently finish scoring opportunities that others typically squander—and that is why they are so valuable to their teams. Not every player, regardless of how hard or long he practices, has the physical and mental capabilities to develop into a top-notch goal scorer. I can state with utmost confidence, however, that virtually every player can sharpen shooting skills and improve the ability to finish scoring chances. In doing so, the athlete can play a more important role in the team's attacking efforts. As a coaching adage so aptly states, "Good luck generally occurs where preparation meets opportunity." The key word here is *preparation*—and that begins with regular practice in well-structured training sessions.

The shooting games described in this chapter will expose your players to the competitive pressures they'll face in game situations—pressures such as restricted space, limited time, physical fatigue, and determined opponents challenging for the ball. You can modify the exercises to emphasize the scoring technique of your choice. You can also easily adapt the exercises to make them more or less difficult by adjusting variables such as area size, number of touches permitted, and number of players participating.

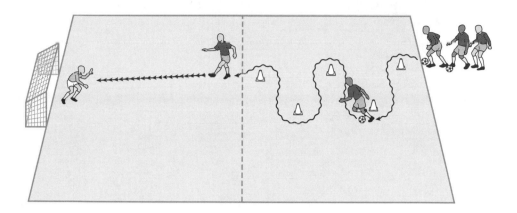

Minutes: 10 to 15

Players: 4 to 6 (3 to 5 shooters and 1 goalkeeper)

Objectives: To shoot with power and accuracy off the dribble; to dribble with close control in tight spaces; to provide goalkeeper training

Setup: Use markers to form a rectangular field area 30 yards wide by 40 yards long, divided by a midline. Position a regulation goal at the midpoint of one end line. Shooters, each with a ball, stand at the opposite end line. Use discs or flags to represent five small goals, arranged in a zigzag pattern, in the half of the field occupied by the shooters. Have a goalkeeper in the regulation goal.

Procedure: Shooters, in turn, dribble at top speed through the five minigoals. After dribbling through the last goal, the shooter pushes the ball into the goalkeeper's half of the field, sprints to it, and then shoots to score. The player immediately retrieves the ball and returns to the starting position. Continue the exercise until each player has attempted 20 shots at goal.

Scoring: Award the shooter 2 points for a goal scored and 1 point for a shot on goal saved by the goalkeeper. The player with the most points wins.

Practice tips: Position the minigoals so that shooters are required to cut the ball sharply and change direction when dribbling through them. Emphasize dribbling speed and close control. With younger players, use fewer minigoals and increase their width.

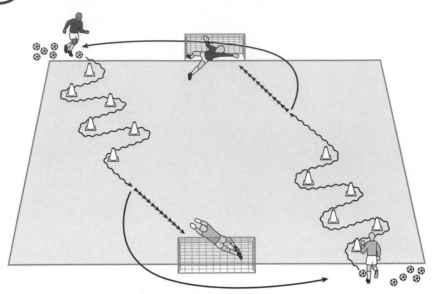

Minutes: 20

Players: 8 to 10 (in pairs plus 2 goalkeepers)

Objectives: To improve ability to shoot off the dribble

Setup: Use markers to outline a field 20 yards wide by 30 yards long. Center a regulation goal on each end line. Players compete against a partner. Partners stand at opposite ends of the field, in the corners diagonally opposite one another. Deposit a supply of balls in each corner. Position a series of markers in front of each partner to create a dribbling obstacle course. Have a goalkeeper in each goal.

Procedure: On the command of "Go," partners dribble through their respective slalom courses, push the ball forward, and shoot on goal to score. After shooting, each player continues to run forward and around the goal, picks up another ball in the corner, and then dribbles though that slalom course and attempts to score. Each partner makes three complete circuits of the field for a total of six shots at goal.

Scoring: The partner who completes three complete circuits in the shortest time is awarded 1 point. Partners are also awarded 1 point for each goal scored, for a possible maximum score of 7 points per round. The player scoring the most points wins the round.

Practice tips: Encourage players to dribble the slalom course at top speed. Once through the course, they should push the ball forward a few strides, sprint to it, and shoot on goal before sprinting around the goal to begin the next slalom.

Minutes: 10 to 15

Players: 3 (2 shooters, 1 goalkeeper)

Objectives: To practice shooting and scoring off the dribble; to compete in a pressure training exercise; to improve fitness

Setup: Play on one end of a regulation field. Players pair for competition. One player stands 35 yards from the goal with a dozen soccer balls. His partner starts at a top corner of the penalty area, 18 yards from the goal. The goalkeeper stands in the goal.

Procedure: On the command of "Go," the player standing 35 yards from the goal dribbles at top speed toward the goal and attempts to score from a distance of 15 yards or greater. If the shooter scores, he immediately returns to the 35-yard spot, collects another ball, and repeats. If the shooter fails to score, then he switches places with his partner at the corner of the penalty area; that player immediately sprints to the 35-yard line, collects a ball, and attempts to score. Continue the exercise until the supply of balls is depleted or a specific time limit expires. Repeat the game several times.

Scoring: The player scoring the most goals wins the Golden Boot award as the top scorer of the tournament

Practice tips: Encourage players to dribble at speed prior to releasing their shot. Players should focus on proper shooting technique, striking the ball on the instep with hips square to the goal.

Minutes: 20 to 25 (series of 5-minute rounds)

Players: 9 to 13 (8 to 12 field players, in pairs plus 1 goalkeeper)

Objective: To improve goal-scoring ability under the gamelike pressures of limited time, restricted space, and challenging opponents

Setup: Play within the penalty area of a regulation field with a full-sized goal centered on the end line. Place a supply of balls inside the goal. Organize pairs of players. Each pair chooses a country to represent (for example, USA, England, Germany). All pairs begin within the penalty area. The neutral goalkeeper starts within the goal.

Procedure: The game begins with the goalkeeper tossing a couple of balls toward the outer edge of the penalty area. Pairs vie for possession. Teams gaining possession of a ball attempt to score in the full-sized goal, while other pairs defend. The offside rule is not in effect. Pairs that do not possess a ball defend, whereas the pairs in possession of a ball immediately attack the goal. After each save or score, the goalkeeper returns the ball into play by tossing it toward the edge of the penalty area. Two balls are kept in play at all times. Players must shout out their country name when they score a goal, or the goal does not count, and they should keep a tally of how many goals they score during the round. Play a series of 4- or 5-minute rounds. The team that scores the most goals through all rounds of the World Cup is declared the World Cup champion.

Scoring: Normal soccer rules apply other than the offside rule; it is waived. All shots must be taken from within the penalty area but outside of the 6-yard goal box.

Practice tips: The focus is on scoring goals under gamelike conditions. Encourage players to shoot at every opportunity, to take on defenders, and to combine with their teammate to create scoring opportunities. Prohibit slide tackles.

Minutes: 15

Players: Unlimited (in groups of 4; 1 shooter, 1 goalkeeper, 2 servers)

Objectives: To develop shooting skills under matchlike pressures; to improve fitness

Setup: Play on one end of a regulation field with a full-sized goal centered on the end line. Designate one player as shooter, one as goalkeeper, and two as servers. The shooter stands 25 yards from the end line, with her back to the goal. The servers begin 30 yards from the goal facing the shooter, with 10 to 12 balls between them. The goalkeeper begins in the goal.

Procedure: One server plays a ball past the shooter, (toward the goal) who quickly turns, sprints to the ball, and shoots to score. The shooter must strike the ball first time (one touch), then immediately sprint back to the start position. The second server immediately plays another ball past the shooter, this time to the opposite side. Continue the exercise until the supply of balls is depleted. The goalkeeper tries to save all shots. The players rotate positions (server or shooter) after each round. Play several rounds.

Scoring: Shooters are awarded 1 point for a shot on goal and 2 points for a goal scored. The player who scores the most points wins the round.

Practice tips: Encourage shooters to get to the ball as quickly as possible, taking the most direct route. Require first-time shots as well as alternate shots with right and left feet. Reduce the shooting distance and the number of repetitions for younger players.

Minutes: 3 per round

Players: 7 (1 shooter, 5 servers, 1 goalkeeper)

Objectives: To improve the ability to shoot with power and accuracy; to improve fitness; to provide goalkeeper training

Setup: Play on one end of a regulation field with a full-sized goal. Place a cone on the front edge of the penalty arc, about 22 yards from the goal. Five servers, each with a supply of balls, stand around the perimeter of the penalty area. The shooter stands on the penalty arc next to the cone. The goalkeeper is within the goal.

Procedure: Server 1 pushes a ball into the penalty area. The shooter moves quickly to the ball, controls it toward the goal with the first touch, and shoots to score with the second touch. The shooter runs back to the cone and then sprints to a ball pushed into the penalty area by server 2. The goalkeeper attempts to save all shots. Continue through the servers for two rounds of shots (10 consecutive shots), after which the shooter switches positions with one of the servers, and the round is repeated with a different shooter. Continue until all players have taken two turns as the shooter.

Scoring: Award 1 point for a shot on goal and 2 points for a goal scored. The player who scores the most points wins.

Practice tips: Vary the type of service (rolling, bouncing, or lofted balls). As a variation, require first-time (one-touch) shooting or add a pressuring defender.

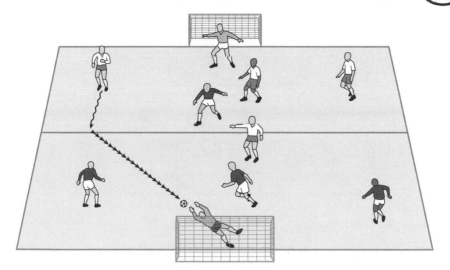

Minutes: 15 to 20

Players: 10 (8 field players, 2 goalkeepers)

Objectives: To improve the ability to shoot from distance; to develop combination play among teammates

Setup: Use markers to extend the length of the sides of the penalty area to twice the normal length, creating a field area 36 yards long and 44 yards wide divided by a midline. Position a full-sized goal on each end line. You'll need one ball per game, plus an extra supply of balls in each goal.

Procedure: Organize two teams of four field players and one goalkeeper. Each team positions three field players and the goalkeeper in its defending half and one player in the opponent's half of the field, creating a 3v1 situation in each half. Players are restricted to movement within their assigned half of the field. Play begins with the goalkeeper distributing the ball to one of the three teammates stationed in the defending half, who then attempt to score on the opposing keeper. The single opponent stationed in that half of the field attempts to prevent shots on his goalkeeper. Players are restricted to three touches or fewer to pass, receive, and shoot the ball. All shots must originate from the team's defending half of the field. The fourth member of the attacking team, positioned in the opposite half, can follow up shots on goal to finish any rebounds that come off the opposing keeper. After each shot at goal or change of possession, the defending goalkeeper restarts play by distributing the ball to a teammate stationed in his team's defending zone.

Scoring: Award 1 point for each shot on goal, 2 points for a goal scored. Team scoring the most points wins.

Practice tips: The 3v1 player advantage in each zone should provide numerous long-range scoring opportunities. Encourage quick ball movement to create open shooting lanes to goal. Emphasize the proper instep shooting technique.

Minutes: 15

Players: 7 to 11 (2 equal-sized teams of 3 to 5 plus 1 neutral goalkeeper)

Objectives: To improve finishing skills; to provide shot-stopping practice for goalkeeper; to improve general endurance

Setup: Use markers to outline an area about 40 yards square. Position two flags or poles in the center of the area to represent a full-sized goal. The neutral goalkeeper stands within the goal. Award one team possession of the ball. Use colored vests to differentiate teams.

Procedure: Begin with a kickoff with the ball spotted along a perimeter line of the area. Teams can score through either side of the central goal, so the goalkeeper must constantly readjust position in response to movement of the ball. After each save, the goalkeeper tosses the ball toward a corner of the playing area, where teams vie for possession. Change of possession occurs after a scored goal, when the ball travels out of the field area, or when a defending player steals the ball. A ball played out-of-bounds is returned by a throw-in. Regular soccer rules are in effect other than the offside rule, which is waived.

Scoring: A shot traveling through the goal below the height of the goalkeeper's head counts as a goal scored. The team scoring the most goals wins.

Practice tips: Place restrictions on players (such as only two-touch or three-touch passes). To increase scoring opportunities, add a neutral player to the game who always joins the team with possession of the ball to create a numerical advantage for the attack.

Minutes: 15

Players: 6 (2 flank players, 2 strikers (shooters), 1 server, and 1 goalkeeper)

Objectives: To improve ability to score off balls served from the flanks

Setup: Play on one-half of a regulation field with a full-sized goal on the end line. Position two wingers (flank players) together near to the halfway line, approximately 10 yards in from one sideline. The wingers will alternate turns serving balls into the goal area. Have two shooters (strikers) begin near the front edge of the penalty area. The goalkeeper stands in the goal. A server is in the center circle with a supply of balls.

Procedure: The server plays a ball into the space between the flank players and the end line. One flank player runs onto the ball, dribbles forward several yards at full speed, and crosses the ball into the goal area. The two strikers stagger their runs (one toward near post, one toward far post) to get on the end of a serve and strike first time on goal. After each attempt, the strikers return to their original starting positions. The server then plays a ball into open space for the second flank player, and the drill is repeated. Continue the drill, alternating crosses from one flank player and then the other, until the supply of balls is depleted. After the round is completed, return all balls to the server and repeat the drill from the opposite flank.

Scoring: Award 1 point for a shot on goal saved by the goalkeeper; award 2 points for goal scored. The player totaling the most points wins the competition.

Practice tips: Encourage shooters to time their runs into the goal area so they arrive at the same time the ball is served into the area. This game is appropriate for experienced players who have the ability to serve the ball from the flanks into the goal area.

Minutes: 15 to 20

Players: Unlimited (in pairs plus 1 or 2 goalkeepers who alternate turns in the goal)

Objectives: To improve individual ability to score in a breakaway situation

Setup: Play on one end of a regulation field with a full-sized goal centered on the end line. Use markers to designate a line parallel to the end line at a distance of approximately 35 yards from goal. Pair players with a partner for competition; one ball required per pair.

Procedure: Partners (A and B) line up side by side on the 35-yard line; A has the ball. Player A pushes the ball forward toward the goal about 10 yards and sprints to it. Player B remains on the 35-yard line until the ball has been touched again by A, then sprints forward to chase and prevent A from scoring on a breakaway. A must dribble into the penalty area before releasing a shot on goal. Players rotate roles after each attempt on goal and repeat.

Scoring: Award the shooter 1 point for each goal scored. The player scoring the most points after 25 repetitions wins the game.

Practice tips: Encourage the shooter to dribble at top speed toward the goal so the chasing defender cannot catch up. To do so, the dribbler must take the most direct route to the goal and release the shot at the most opportune moment.

Minutes: 10

Players: 3 (2 shooters, 1 goalkeeper)

Objectives: To develop the ability to shoot with power and accuracy off the volley

Setup: Position two markers about 25 yards from goal, about 10 yards apart. Place five or six balls at each marker.

Procedure: One shooter stands at each marker to begin. On the command of "Go," one shooter picks up a ball, tosses it upward toward the goal, sprints forward, allows the ball to bounce once, and then volleys on goal. The shooter immediately sprints back to the marker, picks up another ball, and repeats the action until her supply of balls has been depleted. The second shooter then takes her turn at volleying to score.

Scoring: Award 1 point for each shot on goal and 2 points for a goal scored. Play several rounds with a short rest period between rounds. The player totaling the most points wins the competition.

Practice tips: Emphasize correct shooting technique while performing the drill at game speed. Require each shooter to alternate shots with left and right feet. To increase pressure on the shooters, position two additional players as servers, who toss balls from various angles and locations.

Minutes: 20

Players: 10 to 14 (2 teams of 5 to 7 players each)

Objectives: To develop the ability to score off a rolling ball coming directly toward the shooter; to generate competition and enthusiasm in a shooting session

Setup: Play on one end of a regulation field with a full-sized goal on the end line. Divide the group into two teams. Team 1 players begin next to one goalpost; team 2 players begin at the other goal post. Place a marker 18 yards front and center of the goal. Each team has a supply of soccer balls nearby.

Procedure: To begin, one player from team 1 stands in the goal. The first player in line for team 2 sprints out from the goalpost, around the marker 18 yards from goal, and then turns toward the goal. At that moment, the second player in line for team 2 plays a rolling ball toward the penalty spot for his teammate to finish with a one-time shot. After the player shoots to score, he sprints to the goal line and becomes the goalkeeper while team 1 attempts to score in the same manner. If the player from team 2 fails to get to the goal in time, the opposing shooter has an empty net to shoot at; hence the game name. Teams compete for a predetermined time or number of goals scored.

Scoring: Each goal scored counts 1 point. The team scoring the most goals wins the game.

Practice tips: You can vary the type of service (rolling balls, bouncing balls, angled passes, and so on) depending upon the focus of the scoring session.

Minutes: 15 to 20

Players: 6 (3 attackers, 1 defender, 1 goalkeeper, 1 server)

Objectives: To practice shooting skills under the pressures of limited time and a challenging opponent; to provide goalkeeper training

Setup: Play within the penalty area of a regulation field. Designate three players as attackers, one player as the defender, and one player as the server. The goalkeeper is in goal. The server stands outside of the penalty area restraining arc with a supply of 10 to 12 balls.

Procedure: The server begins play by passing the ball to one of the attackers. The three attackers play two-touch soccer in an attempt to beat the defender and shoot to score. If the shooter scores, the server immediately plays another ball into the attackers, and the defender continues as the defender. A shooter fails to score if: a shot goes wide or over the goal, she takes more than two touches, she loses possession, or the goalkeeper makes a save. The player who fails to score immediately becomes the defender and the original defender joins the attack.

Scoring: The player scoring the most goals wins the competition.

Practice tips: You can vary the number of touches permitted to the attackers to increase or decrease the difficulty of scoring goals. You can also add a second defender to the drill.

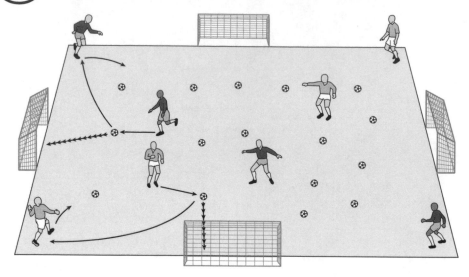

Minutes: 20 minutes (a series of minicompetitions)

Players: 8 (2 teams of 4)

Objectives: To incorporate fitness training with shooting exercises; to improve the ability to strike a set piece on goal

Setup: Use markers to outline a 50-yard-square area. Place a portable goal at the midpoint of each sideline and end line. Distribute 16 to 20 balls at various locations within the central area of the field. All balls should placed at least 15 yards from any goal. Organize two teams of four players each. Have two players from each team begin within the field area; the two remaining players for each team start in a corner of the field area. No goalkeepers required.

Procedure: On your command, the competition begins. The two pairs of players stationed within the field area compete against one another by shooting balls at any of the four goals. After each shot on goal, the shooters must sprint to the corner of the field and tag a teammate; the player who is tagged immediately sprints into the field to shoot a ball while his teammate rests in the corner. Competition continues with teammates alternating shots at goal until the supply of balls has been depleted.

Scoring: Players keep a total of how many goals they score. The team totaling the most goals wins the game. Play a series of games.

Practice tips: You can vary the size of the field area to increase or decrease the physical demands of the game. You can also impose restrictions on shooters; for example, you might require the shooter to dribble the ball at least five yards before shooting at goal.

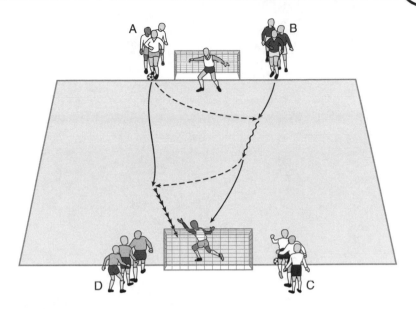

Minutes: 15

Players: 14 (4 groups of 3 plus 2 goalkeepers)

Objectives: To improve shooting accuracy and power; to attack in combination with a teammate

Setup: Use markers to outline a 30-yard-wide by 40-yard-long field. Center a regulation goal on each end line. Organize four groups (A, B, C, and D) of three players each; position one group next to each goalpost. Groups A and B are on the same end line; groups C and D on the opposite end line. Group A is diagonally opposite group C, and group B is diagonally opposite group D. Station a goalkeeper in each goal.

Procedure: The first player in group A passes to the first player in group B and then sprints forward toward the opposite goal. The B player receives the ball, dribbles forward 8 to 10 yards, and then passes the ball into the path of the A player, who receives the ball with the first touch and shoots on goal with the second touch. The B player follows up the shot to collect a possible rebound off the goalkeeper. Immediately after attempting to score, players go to the end of the lines directly opposite their starting point. The first two players in groups C and D repeat the exercise toward the opposite goal; the C player starts the action by passing to the D player. Continue the exercise for 15 continuous minutes.

Scoring: Award 1 point for a shot on goal; 2 points for a goal scored. The player totaling the most points wins the competition.

Practice tips: Encourage players to perform the exercise at game speed, even though defenders are not involved. As a variation, have the passer loft balls into the path of the shooter, thus requiring volley shots.

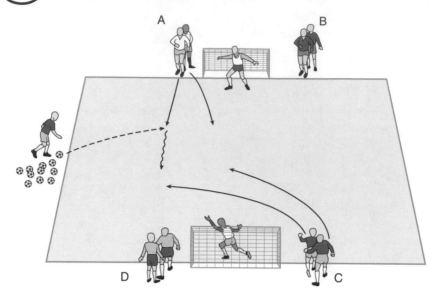

Minutes: 20 minutes (series of 2-minute games)

Players: 11 (4 teams of 2 plus 2 goalkeepers and 1 server)

Objectives: To combine with a teammate to create scoring opportunities; to develop shooting skills under gamelike pressures; to provide goalkeeper training; to improve fitness

Setup: Use markers to outline a 30-yard-wide by 40-yard-long field. Center a regulation goal on each end line. Organize four teams of two players each. Teams A and B begin on one end line and teams C and D on the opposite end line. Have a goalkeeper in each goal and a server at the midline of the field with a supply of balls.

Procedure: The server kicks a ball into the field area; teams A and C enter the field from opposite end lines and compete for the ball. The team gaining possession attempts to score in the opponent's goal while the opponents defend. Roles immediately reverse upon change of possession. After a shot on goal, a score, or a ball out of play, the server immediately serves another ball into the area, and the game continues. Play nonstop for 2 minutes; then teams B and D replace A and C and repeat the drill. Play a series of 2-minute games.

Scoring: Each goal scored counts 1 point. The team scoring the most goals wins the round.

Practice tips: Encourage players to attack at speed and to shoot at every opportunity. To keep players active the entire time, a large supply of balls is required.

Minutes: 20

Players: 12 (2 teams of 5 field players plus 2 goalkeepers)

Objectives: To develop the ability to shoot with power and accuracy from outside the penalty area; to improve general endurance; to provide goalkeeper training

Setup: Use markers to form a rectangular field area 40 yards wide by 60 yards long. Position a regulation goal at the midpoint of each end line. Use markers to further divide the field into three equal 20- by 40-yard zones. Organize two teams of five field players and one goalkeeper. Each team defends a goal. Award one team the ball to begin.

Procedure: Begin with a kickoff from the center of the field. All shots must originate from within the middle zone, 20 yards or more from the goal; otherwise, regular soccer rules apply. Players are permitted to score from within the end zones but only off a rebound off the goalkeeper or goal post.

Scoring: Award 3 points for a goal scored and 1 point for a shot on goal saved by the goalkeeper. The team scoring the most points wins.

Practice tips: Adjust the area size to the ages and abilities of your players. For example, require players under 13 to take shots from a distance of 15 yards or greater.

Minutes: 15 to 20 (series of 90-second rounds)

Players: 4 (2 shooters, 1 server, 1 goalkeeper)

Objectives: To practice finishing skills under gamelike pressures of restricted space and physical fatigue; to improve fitness; to provide goalkeeper training

Setup: Play on one end of a regulation field with a full-sized goal on the end line. Partner two players for competition; both players begin within the penalty area. Position a server at the top (front edge) of the penalty area with a dozen balls. The goalkeeper stands in the common goal.

Procedure: To begin, the server plays a ball into the penalty area, where both players vie for possession. The player gaining possession attempts to score; the opponent defends. The keeper attempts to save all shots. Players switch roles (attack to defense and vice versa) upon each change of possession. Play stops momentarily after a goal is scored, when the goalkeeper makes a save, or when the ball is kicked out of bounds. The server immediately restarts play by kicking another ball into the area. Continue nonstop until the supply of balls is used up. Repeat the round with a different pair of players competing within the penalty area.

Scoring: The player scoring the most goals wins the round. Play a series of rounds with a brief rest between rounds.

Practice tips: Players must recognize scoring opportunities and release shots at any chance. Emphasize quick release and accuracy rather than pure power.

Minutes: 20

Players: 12 (2 teams of 5 players plus 2 goalkeepers)

Objectives: To develop the ability to score through combination play; to improve the ability to score under gamelike pressures

Setup: Use markers to outline a field area of 60 yards long by 40 yards wide bisected by a midline. Create two teams of five field players and a goalkeeper. Position a regulation goal at the center of each end line. Designate three attackers and two defenders for each team. Attackers play in the opponent's half of the field; defenders play in their own team's half (closest to the goal they are defending). This setup creates a 3v2 situation in each half of the field. Assign a goalkeeper to each goal; use colored vests to differentiate teams. Award one goalkeeper possession of the ball to begin.

Procedure: The goalkeeper starts play by distributing the ball to a teammate in the opposite half of the field. Each team defends a goal and tries to score in the opponent's goal. Attackers and defenders are restricted to their designated half of the field. A defender who wins the ball initiates a counterattack by passing to a teammate (attacker) in the opposite half of the field. After each save, the goalkeeper distributes the ball to a teammate in the opposite half of the field. A team scored against is awarded possession of the ball to restart play.

Scoring: The team scoring the most goals wins the game.

Practice tips: As a variation, impose restrictions. For example, require three-touch passing only, or allow scoring off first-time shots only. This game is most appropriate for mature players who have the skill and experience to successfully combine with teammates.

Minutes: 20 to 25

Players: 8 to 12 (2 equal-sized teams of 4 to 6)

Objectives: To score off volley shots; to develop general endurance

Setup: Use markers to outline a rectangular playing area 60 yards long by 40 yards wide. Position a full-sized goal on the center of each end line. Form two teams of equal numbers. Award one team the ball to begin. Use colored vests to differentiate teams. Goalkeepers are not required.

Procedure: Each team defends a goal. Players pass the ball to one another by throwing (and catching) rather than kicking. A player may take no more than five steps with the ball before releasing it to a teammate. Change of possession occurs when an opposing player intercepts a pass, a ball that goes out of play was last touched by an attacking player, the ball is dropped to the ground, a player takes more than five steps with the ball, or a goal is scored. Points are scored by volleying a ball tossed by a teammate through the opponent's goal. Players are *not* permitted to toss the ball to themselves to volley into the goal. Although goalkeepers are not used, all players are permitted to use their hands to catch the ball and block passes or shots.

Scoring: The team scoring the most goals wins.

Practice tips: Encourage teammates to move up and down the field as a compact unit, supporting one another and making themselves available for passes. Since full-volley shots require precise timing and correct technique to execute, this game may not be appropriate for young or inexperienced players.

Minutes: 20

Players: 14 (2 teams of 6 plus 2 goalkeepers)

Objectives: To practice attacking at speed in numbers-up situations; to defend when outnumbered

Setup: Play on a 30-yard-long by 20-yard-wide field with a full-sized goal centered on each end line (goals A and B). Place a goalkeeper in each goal. Organize two teams (team 1 and team 2) of six players each. Use colored vests to differentiate teams. To begin, position two players from team 2 to defend goal B. Have team 1 and the remaining players from team 2 begin on the same end line, one team to each side of goal A. Place a supply of balls inside each goal. Team 1 has the ball to begin.

Procedure: Three players from team 1 advance off the end line to attack goal B, defended by two players from team 2 and a goalkeeper. Immediately after a shot on goal, a shot traveling over the end line, or a ball stolen by a defender, the goalkeeper in goal B distributes a ball to the original two defenders (team 2), who immediately attack goal A. One of the three original attackers from team 1 drops back to defend goal A, creating a 2v1 player advantage for team 2 as they counterattack on goal A. The other two attackers from team 1 remain near the end line (goal B) to defend goal B in the next round. Immediately after an attempt on goal A, three players from team 2 advance off the line to attack goal B, which is now defended by two players from team 1. The game continues back and forth, with a 3v2 attack on goal B, and a 2v1 counterattack on goal A.

Scoring: Award 1 point for each goal scored. The team scoring the most goals wins the game.

Practice tips: Emphasize an immediate transition between attack and defense.

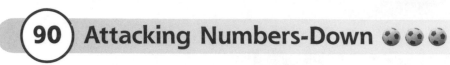

Minutes: 20

Players: 8 (3 teams of 2, 1 neutral player, and 1 goalkeeper)

Objectives: To penetrate when attacking in a numbers-down (fewer players) situation; to practice scoring under gamelike pressures; to develop endurance

Setup: Play on one end of a regulation field with a full-sized goal centered on the end line. Form three teams of two players each. Start all teams within the penalty area, along with a neutral player who plays with the team in possession. Use colored vests to differentiate teams. The goalkeeper stands within the goal. You'll need one ball per game; place extra balls within the goal.

Procedure: The goalkeeper begins play by tossing the ball outside the penalty area, where all three teams vie for possession. The team winning the ball attacks the goal; the other two teams defend. The neutral player joins the team in possession to create a 3v4 attacking situation. If a defending player steals the ball, his team immediately switches to attack and tries to score. The goalkeeper attempts to save all shots. After a goal or goalkeeper save, or if the ball goes out of play, the goalkeeper continues play by tossing the ball outside of the penalty area, where teams again vie for possession.

Scoring: Award 1 point for a shot on goal and 2 points for a goal scored. The team scoring the most points wins.

Practice tips: The outnumbered (3v4) attacking team should attempt to isolate defending players by using one- and two-touch passes combined with creative dribbling. The give-and-go (wall) pass is also an effective tactic when attacking numbers-down.

CHAPTER 6

Heading Games

Soccer is the only sport in which players literally use their head to propel the ball. The ability to head the ball with power and accuracy has become increasingly important in the modern game where defenses are highly organized to prevent opponents from penetrating via the pass or dribble. In those instances, serving the ball over a block of defending players can be an effective means of creating scoring opportunities through the air. That said, mastery of the air game is essential for all field players, because heading skills can be used for both attacking and defending purposes. Three techniques are commonly used; each is featured in a specific situation and for a slightly different purpose.

The *jump header* technique is typically used when leaping above an opponent who is also trying to head the ball. The player uses a two-footed takeoff to jump up, arches the upper body back, and then snaps forward at the waist to contact the ball on the flat surface of the forehead. Scoring opportunities can originate from balls crossed from the flank, corner kicks, free kicks, and long throw-ins. The ball should be headed on a downward plane toward the goal line when attempting to score, because that is the most difficult save for the goalkeeper.

A slightly different technique is used for defending purposes, such as when attempting to clear a ball that is flighted into your goal area. In these situations the ball should be headed high, far, and preferably toward the flank area of the field, away from the most dangerous scoring zone front and center of the goal. Such a clearance denies opponents an immediate strike at goal and also provides defending players time to reorganize.

The *dive header* is an acrobatic skill that can be used to score off a low-driven ball traveling across the goal area or to clear the opponent's crosses out of the goal area. To execute this maneuver, the player dives parallel to the ground with the head held firm and tilted back. The ball is contacted on the flat surface of the forehead, with arms and hands extended downward to break the fall to the ground.

The *flicked header* is a third option, designed to alter the flight path of the ball while allowing it to continue in the same direction. This technique is most often used in attacking situations to alter the trajectory of a driven ball. To execute the flicked header, a player moves into a position to intercept the ball's flight path, angles the forehead back, and allows the ball to glance off the top of the forehead. This action will create a sudden change in the ball's flight trajectory, which can pose problems for defending players.

The heading games described in this chapter can be adapted for practicing all of the aforementioned heading techniques, depending on the focus of the training session. At the youth level of competition (12 years and under) heading is probably the least frequently used skill. Passing, receiving, and shooting skills occur far more often in the course of play, so the youth coach need not devote much practice time to the development of heading skills. As players mature and advance to higher levels of play, however, the ability to head the ball with power and accuracy becomes more important in determining the outcome of a match. The amount of emphasis on heading skills during training sessions should reflect this fact. The practice of heading skills should not be a priority for players 10 and younger, although for safety reasons they should at least be introduced to proper heading technique.

Players should face the oncoming ball with shoulders square. As the ball arrives, they should use a two-footed takeoff to jump up, with the upper trunk arched back from the waist, the chin tucked toward the chest, and the neck firm. They should then snap the upper trunk forward from the waist and contact the ball on the flat surface of the forehead just above the eyebrows. Remind youngsters to keep their eyes open (watch the ball!) and mouth closed as the ball contacts the forehead. It is not uncommon for young players to have difficulty coordinating the timing of the jump with proper heading technique, so it is best to introduce the skill in stages, first teaching them to head the ball while keeping their feet on the ground and later, as they become more proficient, progressing to jumping and heading.

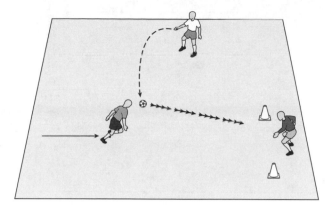

Minutes: 10

Players: Unlimited (in groups of 3)

Objective: To develop the heading technique used to score goals

Setup: Position markers to form an area 10 yards by 15 yards for each group. Use flags to represent a goal 4 yards wide on one end of the area. Have one player in the goal as goalkeeper, one player to the side of the goal to be server, and one player 8 yards front and center of the goal as the header. One ball is required.

Procedure: The server tosses the ball upward so that it drops near the center of the area. The header judges the ball's flight, moves forward, and attempts to score by heading the ball through the goal past the goalkeeper. Players rotate positions after each header and repeat. Play for 10 continuous minutes.

Scoring: Award 2 points for a goal scored and 1 point for a header on goal saved by the keeper. The player who scores the most points at the end of the game wins.

Practice tips: Encourage players to jump early, hang in the air, and head the ball downward toward a corner of the goal. Emphasize proper heading form (upper body arched back from the vertical, chin tucked, neck stiff, ball contacted on forehead). Allow beginning players to head the ball with both feet on the ground; require advanced players to jump and head the ball.

Minutes: 10

Players: Unlimited (in groups of 3)

Objectives: To improve jump header technique; to improve leg strength and power

Setup: Two players (servers 1 and 2) stand 10 yards apart, each with a ball. A third player stands midway between the servers.

Procedure: Server 1 tosses a ball upward toward the central player, slightly above head height. The central player jumps upward and heads the ball directly back to the server and then immediately turns 180 degrees to jump and head a ball tossed by server 2. Continue at maximum speed for 30 consecutive headers, after which the central player exchanges places with one of the servers. Repeat the exercise until each player has taken a minimum of two turns as the header.

Scoring: Award 1 point for each ball headed directly back to the server's chest. The player scoring the most points wins.

Practice tips: Players should jump vertically upward (not forward), arch the upper trunk back before the ball's arrival, and then snap forward to contact the ball with the forehead. Encourage players to keep the head steady with eyes open and mouth closed as they contact the ball. Younger players can head the ball while keeping their feet on the ground.

Minutes: 15

Players: Unlimited (in pairs)

Objective: To develop jump header technique

Setup: Pair players for heading competition. Use markers to form one rectangular area 10 by 12 yards for each pair. Position flags or cones or discs as goals at each end. Players stand in opposite goals, facing each another. Player 1 has the ball to begin play.

Procedure: Player 1 tosses the ball upward so it drops near the center of the area. Player 2 moves forward from his goal line, jumps up, and attempts to score by heading the ball past player 1 through the goal. Players return to their respective goals after each header and switch roles. Repeat 50 times with each player attempting 25 headers on goal.

Scoring: Award 1 point for each goal scored. The player who scores the most points wins.

Practice tips: To head the ball with power, encourage players to arch the upper trunk back at the waist and snap the upper body forward to contact the ball. They should keep the neck and head firm at the moment of contact.

Minutes: 10

Players: Unlimited (in equal-sized teams of 4 to 6)

Objective: To improve heading technique

Setup: Teams line up side by side in single file. Maintain at least three yards between teams. One player for each team functions as the server and stands two yards in front of the team, facing the first player in line. Each server has a ball.

Procedure: On your command, servers toss a ball at head height to the first player in their line, who heads it back to the server and immediately drops to his knees. The server catches the ball and immediately tosses to the second player in line, who also heads and then kneels. Servers continue through the team until all players have headed and are kneeling. The team whose players are all kneeling first wins the race. Players on each team then stand and rotate positions in preparation for the next round. The original server moves to the back of the line, the first player in line becomes the server, and everyone else moves one spot forward.

Scoring: The first team to win six races wins the competition.

Practice tips: While players should complete the heading race as quickly as possible, they should not sacrifice proper heading technique for speed. Encourage players to focus on correct heading technique at all times.

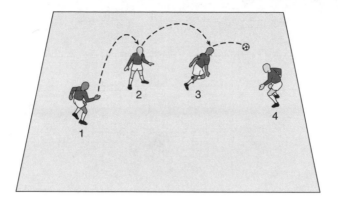

Minutes: 5 to 10

Players: Unlimited (in teams of 4)

Objectives: To practice the correct technique of heading the ball off the flat surface of the forehead

Setup: Organize teams of four players each. Each team stands within an area 10 yards by 10 yards. One ball is required per team.

Procedure: The player with the ball tosses it upward in the air toward a teammate to begin the game. Teammates must then keep the ball in the air for as many touches as possible, using only their heads to keep the ball airborne. If the ball drops to the ground, the team must restart the count at zero. The team that keeps the ball airborne for the most consecutive headers wins the game.

Scoring: Each team totals all its consecutive headers. The team with the most consecutive headers wins the competition.

Practice tips: Players should contact the ball with the flat surface of the forehead, directing the ball toward a teammate who then continues the heading circuit. Players should bend at the knees slightly and keep their eyes open and mouths closed as they head the ball.

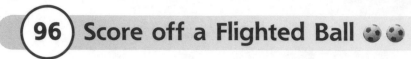

Minutes: 10

Players: 9 (4 teams of 2 players each plus 1 goalkeeper)

Objectives: To practice scoring off balls served into the goal area.

Setup: Play on one end of a regulation field with a full-sized goal on the end line. Players pair with a teammate to create two-player teams. One player from each team begins as a server behind a full-sized goal, with a ball at her feet. Her partner stands on the opposite side facing the goal, near the edge of the penalty area. The neutral goalkeeper positions in goal.

Procedure: To begin, a server chips the ball over the crossbar into the penalty area. Her partner sprints forward and attempts to score by heading the ball directly out of the air into the goal. The play is dead if the ball fails to clear the crossbar, does not drop into the penalty area, or bounces before it is headed on goal. Partners switch places after each attempt. Each pair, in turn, attempts score off of a header. Continue for 10 minutes of serving and heading to score.

Scoring: Each goal scored counts as 1 point. The pair with the most points after 10 minutes wins the game.

Practice tips: This game is not appropriate for younger players who do not have the ability to chip the ball over the crossbar and into the penalty area.

Minutes: 10

Players: Unlimited (in groups of 3 plus 1 server)

Objectives: To practice the technique of defensive heading (clearing a ball high and far)

Setup: Use markers to designate two parallel end lines approximately 10 yards apart and approximately 10 yards in length. One player stands between the lines, in the middle zone, and the other two players cover each of the end zones; the server has a supply of balls to the side of the field.

Procedure: The server tosses a high ball toward one of the end zone players who attempts to head (clear) the ball over the middle zone to the player in the opposite end zone. Players then rotate zones and repeat. Continue for a predetermined time or number of headers for each player.

Scoring: A ball headed completely over the middle zone so that the player in the opposite end zone can receive it out of the air scores 1 point. The player who totals the most points wins the competition.

Practice tips: When clearing a ball, players should attempt to clear the ball high and far, aiming away from an imaginary goal area.

Minutes: 15

Players: Unlimited (2 equal-sized teams)

Objectives: To improve player ability to score off jump headers and dive headers

Setup: Play on one end of a regulation field with a full-sized goal on the end line. Divide the group into two teams, A and B. Team A players line up at one goalpost and team B players at the other goal post. Each team has a supply of soccer balls nearby.

Procedure: One player from team B starts in the goal. Team A then begins the competition. The first team A player in line sprints outward from the goalpost, around the penalty spot (12 yards front and center of goal), then turns and sprints toward goal. As he approaches the goal, the second player in team A line tosses a lofted ball 8 to 10 yards front and center of the goal for his teammate to score via a header. Immediately the player who headed the ball sprints to the goal line and becomes the goalkeeper. Team B then attempts to score in the same manner. Teams compete for a predetermined time or number of goals scored.

Scoring: Each ball headed past the goalkeeper counts as 1 point. The team scoring the most points wins the competition.

Practice tips: You can vary the type of header (for instance, require dive headers only, jump headers only, and so on).

Minutes: 10 to 15 (or time needed to play to a predetermined number of points)

Players: Unlimited (in teams of 3 to 5 plus 2 servers and 1 goalkeeper)

Objective: To develop the ability to score acrobatic goals using the diving header technique

Setup: Play on one end of a regulation field with a full-sized goal centered on the end line. Divide the group into teams of equal numbers. Have the teams line up single file next to one another, about 15 yards from the goal. Have a server 6 yards to each side of the goal, about 6 yards out from the end line. Each server has a supply of balls. The neutral goalkeeper plays within the goal.

Procedure: Servers alternate tossing balls with a trajectory parallel to the ground into the area 8 to 10 yards front and center of the goal. Tosses should be 3 to 4 feet high. Players alternate attempting to score off diving headers by sprinting forward and launching themselves through the air to meet the ball. The goalkeeper attempts to save all shots. Continue the exercise until each player has attempted at least 8 diving headers.

Scoring: Award 2 points for a goal scored and 1 point for a ball on goal saved by the goalkeeper. The team scoring the most points wins.

Practice tips: Dive headers are especially fun to practice on a wet, soggy field. Correct technique is essential to prevent injury. Encourage players to dive forward parallel to the ground with the head tilted back and neck firm. The ball is contacted on the flat surface of the forehead, with eyes open and mouth closed. Arms and hands should extend down to cushion the impact with the ground. This game is not recommended for younger players (10 years and under) who lack adequate strength and coordination.

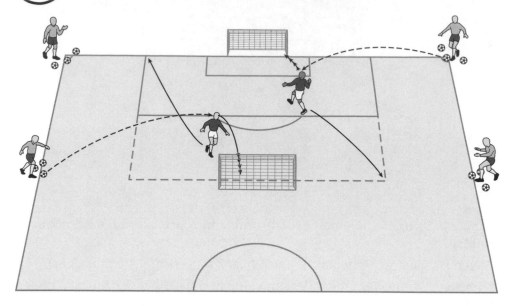

Minutes: 20 (series of 2-minute rounds)

Players: 6 (4 servers and 2 heading players)

Objectives: To improve the ability to score headers from balls served from wide areas; to improve fitness in a competitive heading game

Setup: Play on one end of a regulation field. Use markers to extend the penalty area to twice its depth (to 36 yards); position a regulation goal on each end of the extended penalty area. Have one server at each corner of the field, each with four or five soccer balls. The heading players begin at opposite ends of the playing area, near each goal.

Procedure: On the command of "Go," the heading players sprint forward toward the opposite goals. When they enter the opposite half of the field, one of the servers at that end lofts a ball into the goal area for the player to head and attempt a direct score. After attempting to score off a header, the players immediately turn and sprint toward the opposite goal (their original starting point) to repeat the action. Continue the game until all of the balls have been served; at that point, the central (heading) players switch positions with two servers, and the game is repeated. Continue until all players have taken a turn heading on goal.

Scoring: Each goal scored with the head is 1 point. The player scoring the most goals wins the round.

Practice tips: Encourage players to perform the game at maximum speed and intensity to derive fitness benefits from the game as well as improve their heading technique. If servers struggle to serve accurate balls, narrow the field and have servers toss the balls into the goal area from the flanks.

Minutes: 15

Players: 8 (3 attackers, 2 defenders, 2 servers, 1 goalkeeper)

Objectives: To improve the ability to score off balls crossed from the flanks; to provide goalkeeper training on lofted balls served into the goal area

Setup: Play on one end of a regulation field with a full-sized goal on the end line. Organize a three-player attacking team and a two-player defending team, and have the goalkeeper stand in the goal. Begin with a server on each sideline of the field, about 15 yards from the end line, with a supply of balls.

Procedure: The three-player attacking team starts at the top edge of the penalty area. The two defenders begin at about the penalty spot. Play begins as one of the servers dribbles a ball 8 to 10 yards toward the end line and then serves a lofted pass into the area front and center of the goal. The three attackers attempt to score by heading the ball past the goalkeeper; the defenders attempt to clear the ball out of the goal area. After each attempt, all players return to their original positions and repeat. Servers alternate turns driving balls into the goal area. After a predetermined number of repetitions, have defenders and attackers switch roles.

Scoring: Award 1 point for each goal scored. The group of three that scores the most goals off headers wins the competition.

Practice tips: This game encompasses many of the pressures players will experience in an actual game (for example, defenders contesting for the ball), so the degree of difficulty is quite high. It is not an appropriate game for younger players who do not have the skill or strength to serve balls from the flanks into the goal area.

Minutes: 15

Players: 10 to 12 (2 equal-sized teams)

Objectives: To improve the ability to score by heading; to involve heading skills in a group activity

Setup: Play on a square field area. Position markers to represent six minigoals, each 4 yards wide, spaced randomly within the field area. Form two teams of equal numbers differentiated by colored vests. Award one team the ball to begin. Do not use goalkeepers.

Procedure: Teams can score through either side of all six goals and must defend all six goals. Passing and receiving among teammates are accomplished by tossing and catching, rather than kicking, the ball. Players on the team with possession of the ball are restricted to five or fewer steps before releasing the ball to a teammate. Loss of possession to the opposition occurs if a player takes more than five steps with the ball, if the ball drops to the ground, or if a defending player intercepts a pass. All goals must be scored from dive headers.

Scoring: The team scoring the most goals wins the game.

Practice tips: Emphasize proper dive header technique. Players should dive forward to meet the ball with the head tilted back, neck firm, and head steady. The ball is contacted on the flat surface of the forehead. Hands and arms are extended downward to cushion the fall to ground. This game is appropriate for older, experienced players only.

Minutes: 15

Players: 12 to 16 (2 teams of 4 to 6 plus 4 neutral players)

Objective: To score from headers and develop endurance

Setup: Use markers to form a rectangular area 40 yards wide by 50 yards long. Put a minigoal approximately 4 yards wide at the midpoint of each end line. Organize two teams of four to six players each. Designate four additional neutral players; they always join the team with possession of the ball. Use colored vests to differentiate teams and neutral players. Award one team possession of the ball to begin. No goalkeepers are required.

Procedure: Each team defends a goal and can score in the opponent's goal. Pass the ball by throwing and catching rather than kicking. Players may take up to four steps with the ball before passing it to a teammate. Violation of the four-step rule results in loss of possession to the opposing team. Neutral players join the team in possession to create a four-player advantage for the attack. There are no goalkeepers, but all players may intercept passes or block shots with their hands. Points are scored by heading a ball tossed by a teammate through the opponent's goal. Defending players gain possession of the ball when they intercept an opponent's pass, when an opponent drops the ball to the ground, when an opponent takes more than four steps with the ball, or when the ball is played out of bounds by an opponent.

Scoring: The team scoring the most points wins.

Practice tips: Player movement should simulate the patterns (positioning) used in an actual soccer game. Team members should attack and defend as a group. Players should position themselves at wide angles to the teammate with the ball to create clear passing lanes. Emphasize proper heading technique. Players should head the ball on a downward plane toward the goal line when attempting to score. This game is most appropriate for older, experienced players who have developed adequate heading skills.

Minutes: 20

Players: 10 (2 teams of 5)

Objectives: To improve the ability to finish crosses by heading; to practice serving balls from the flanks

Setup: Play on a 60-yard-long by 50-yard-wide field area with a full-sized goal positioned at the center of each end line. Organize two teams of five players each. Each team defends a goal and can score via headers in the opponent's goal. Award one team possession of the ball to begin. Do not use goalkeepers.

Procedure: Regular soccer rules are in effect. The team with possession attacks the opponent's goal; the defending team defends with two players only (the other three team members move to the sides of the field), to create a 5v2 player advantage for the attacking team. The attacking team must score via headers on balls crossed from either flank, or on flighted balls lofted into the goal area from distance. After each attempt on goal or goal scored, a change of possession occurs, and the former attacking team defends its goal with two players (a different pair is selected each time a team plays defense). Play for 20 minutes.

Scoring: Each score off a header is worth 1 point. The team scoring the most points wins the game.

Practice tips: Encourage players to attack the wide spaces and then serve balls into the goal areas. Attacking players should time their runs into the goal area to meet crosses from their teammates. Add goalkeepers to make scoring more difficult.

CHAPTER 7

Individual and Small-Group Tactical Games

Soccer tactics involve decision making, problem solving, and playing in combination with teammates. Decisions such as when to release the ball; where to position in relation to the ball and opponents; how to defend when outnumbered; and whether to shoot, dribble, or pass in a specific situation are just a few examples of the many choices that confront players during a match. The ability to make good split-second judgments under the pressures of match competition is just as important as being able to perform the skills required in those situations. Players who make appropriate decisions most often have the greatest success.

There are no offensive or defensive specialists in soccer. All field players must defend when the opponents have the ball and contribute to the attack when their team has the ball. More important, players must be willing and able to make an immediate transition from one role to the other. Individual and group attack involves the coordinated involvement of the first, second, and third attackers. The primary objective is to position more attacking players than defending players in the vicinity of the ball to create what is commonly referred to as a numbers-up situation and then exploit that advantage. The player with possession of the ball, the first attacker, is the starting point of attack tactics. The primary role of the second attacker is to provide immediate passing options, or support, for the player on the ball. He plays an important role in executing the give-and-go pass, the double pass, and the takeover maneuvers. The third attacker's job is to provide passing options away from the ball, usually by making penetrating diagonal runs through the defense or overlapping runs behind the defense.

The defending player closest to the ball, commonly referred to as the first defender, is responsible for applying immediate pressure at the point of attack to deny the opposition penetration via the pass or dribble. The second (cover) defender positions to protect the space behind and to the side of the first defender. If the first defender is beaten on the dribble, the covering defender can step forward to close down the dribbler and deny penetration. The second defender is also in position to cut off passes slotted through the space behind the first defender. Third defenders are responsible for protecting the vulnerable space ahead of the ball and behind the second defender, particularly the open area behind the defense on the side of the field opposite the ball.

Tactical training should begin with the most fundamental tactical unit (1v1) and gradually progress to small-group (2v1, 2v2, and 3v2) and eventually larger-group situations. It's important to consider that tactics are of little or no use if players cannot perform basic soccer skills. It would be like trying to teach a motion offense in basketball before players have developed the ability to dribble the ball! For this reason, tactical training should not be emphasized until players are competent in performing fundamental soccer skills. Simply put, younger players should focus on skill development.

The games in this chapter are loosely arranged in a progressive sequence, beginning with individual tactics and progressing through group situations. All games can be adapted to the ages, abilities, and developmental levels of your players. By manipulating factors such as size of the playing area, number of players, types of passes required, number of touches permitted for passing and receiving the ball, and the speed of repetition, you can make the games either more or less challenging for your players.

Minutes: Series of 60-second games (minimum of 5 games)

Players: Unlimited (in pairs)

Objectives: To develop the ability to compete in 1v1 situations; to improve dribbling, tackling, and shielding skills; to improve fitness

Setup: Players pair for competition. Mark off a 15-yard-square playing area for each pair. Use discs or cones to represent a common goal 2 yards wide in the center of the area. One ball required per game.

Procedure: Players compete 1v1 within the area and can score by passing or dribbling the ball through either side of the common goal. Change of possession occurs when the defending player steals the ball, after a goal is scored, or when the ball travels out of the area. Players reverse roles immediately with each change of possession. Play a series of 1-minute games with 30 seconds of rest between games.

Scoring: The player scoring the most points wins.

Practice tips: Increase the size of the goal and shorten the game to 30 seconds for players under 11.

Minutes: 15

Players: Unlimited (in pairs)

Objective: To improve ability to attack and defend in a one-on-one situation

Setup: Players pair up for competition. Use markers to create a 10-yard-wide by 20-yard-long field for each pair. Partners start on opposite end lines facing one another. One player has the ball to begin.

Procedure: Player A, with the ball, serves the ball to player B and immediately moves forward to play as a defender. Player B receives the ball and attempts to beat the defender by dribbling past her and crossing the end line. After a score or change of possession, or when the ball travels out of the field area, both players return to their respective end lines and repeat the round. Partners alternate playing as the defender and attacker.

Scoring: Award 1 point for each score. The player scoring the most points wins the match.

Practice tips: Encourage the attacker to take on the defender at speed, who in turn attempts to deny penetration via the dribble. The defender should quickly close the distance to the attacker after serving the ball and assume the proper defensive posture. Reduce the area size for younger players.

Minutes: 2-minute rounds

Players: 4 per game (2 teams of 2)

Objectives: To improve ability to compete in 1v1 situations; to improve dribbling and tackling skills; to improve fitness

Setup: Organize teams of two. Use markers to create a 15-yard-wide by 20-yard-long playing area for each game. One player on each team becomes a goal by standing on his respective end line. The remaining two players begin in the center of the area. One has the ball to begin; the other defends.

Procedure: The center players compete 1v1. Points are scored by passing the ball to the feet of the opponent's goal. The goals must remain stationary throughout the 2-minute game; they are not permitted to move sideways to receive a passed ball. If the defending player steals the ball, he immediately becomes the attacker and attempts to score in the opponent's goal. Central players are permitted to play the ball back to their teammate (goal) to alleviate pressure and can receive a return pass from the goal player. However, the goal player is not permitted to move forward off the end line in support of his teammate. Change of possession occurs when the defender steals the ball, when the ball travels out of play, and after each point is scored. Play 2-minute rounds after which teammates switch positions; the goalkeeper becomes the field player and vice versa.

Scoring: The player scoring the most goals wins the round. The first team to win five rounds wins the game.

Practice tips: Players acting as goals should have extra soccer balls nearby. When the game ball is kicked out of the area, the goal player can immediately put another ball into play to keep action continuous. As a variation, add sideline support players.

Minutes: Series of 2-minute games

Players: 8 (2 pairs plus 4 supporting defenders)

Objectives: To practice attacking and defending in a 1v1 and 1v2 situation

Setup: Use markers to outline a 30-yard-square field area. Pair players for 1v1 competition. Two pairs begin within the field area to compete simultaneously in 1v1 match-ups. The remaining players stand on the perimeter of the field, one on each of the four sides of the playing area. These players act as supporting defenders. Two soccer balls are required, one for each pair competing within the field area.

Procedure: Competing players sit back to back with the ball next to them. On your command, the games begin. Players leap to their feet and compete for the ball. The player who gains possession (attacker) attempts to score by dribbling across any of the four sides of the playing area. Her opponent (defender) tries to prevent this and is aided by the supporting defender when the attacker attempts to penetrate that side of the square. Sideline (supporting) defenders can move three yards inward off the sideline to challenge an attacker who is dribbling at them, but they may not chase the attacker into the center of the square. When a sideline defender tackles (steals) the ball, she immediately passes it to the defender stationed within the square, who then becomes the attacker. When the defending player stationed within the square steals the ball, she immediately becomes the attacker and attempts to score by dribbling over a sideline. After a score, the attacker dribbles back into the field and play continues. Play for 2 continuous minutes, after which competing players then switch roles with the sideline defenders and begin a new round.

Scoring: Dribbling the ball over a sideline scores 1 point. The player totaling the most points in each 2-minute round wins that round.

Practice tips: You can adjust the field size depending on the age and ability of the players.

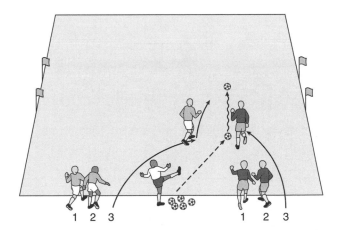

Minutes: 15 minutes

Players: 6 to 8 (in pairs)

Objectives: To improve ability to compete in 1v1 situations; to improve fitness

Setup: Use markers to outline a 25-yard-long by 20-yard-wide field area. Place flags to represent small goals at the midpoint of each 25-yard sideline. Divide players into two equal-sized teams (A and B). Pair each player with an opponent on the opposite team and label those players with the same number (pair 1, pair 2, and so on). Teams line up side by side at one end of the field. The coach stands between the teams, with a supply of balls.

Procedure: The coach serves a ball into the middle of the field and calls out a number, for example, number 1. That pair sprints onto the field and competes for the ball. The player gaining possession can score through either goal by dribbling or passing through the goal. After a score, or if the ball leaves the playing field, the coach serves another ball into the field area and calls the number of a different pair.

Scoring: Award 1 point for each goal scored. Players keep a tally of their points. The team scoring the most points wins the game.

Practice tips: This game requires players to read the pressure of the opponents and to attack the goal least defended. After several rounds, reorganize pairs so players get a chance to compete against different opponents.

Minutes: 15

Players: 7 (3 teams of 2 plus 1 server)

Objectives: To take on and beat an opponent (and, in some cases, two opponents) in tight spaces; to possess the ball under intense defensive pressure; to improve endurance

Setup: Use markers to represent three small goals. Position the goals in the shape of a triangle, with at least 15 yards between them. Organize three teams of two. One member of each team stands outside the triangle, near a goal. The other member of each pair starts within the triangular field area formed by the goals. Have a server to one side of the field with an ample supply of soccer balls.

Procedure: The exercise begins as the server passes a ball into the field. The player who wins the ball (attacker) competes 1v2 against the other middle players (defenders). The attacker can score points by dribbling the ball through any of the three goals. Points may be scored through either side of a goal, but the attacker is not permitted to dribble through the same goal twice in succession. If a defender steals the ball, he immediately becomes the attacker while the original attacker becomes a defender.

Players standing outside the triangle (next to the goals) are passive until their partners tag them. A player who is tagged enters the field and competes; his partner then waits outside of the triangle to rest. Play is continuous.

Scoring: Award 1 point for dribbling through a goal. Keep track of total points scored by each team.

Practice tips: Dribbling is an effective means of penetrating and breaking down a packed defense. Encourage sudden changes of speed and direction coupled with deceptive body feints to beat defenders. Prohibit slide tackles in this game.

Minutes: 15

Players: 5 (2 teams of 2 players each plus 1 neutral goalkeeper)

Objectives: To use dribbling and shielding skills to possess and penetrate the defense; to improve fitness

Setup: Play within the penalty area with a regulation goal on the end line. Form two teams of two players each. Both players from one team begin within the penalty area as defenders. One member of the opposing team also starts within the area as the lone attacker. Her partner begins outside the area as a server, with a supply of balls. The neutral goalkeeper stands in the goal.

Procedure: Play begins with the server kicking a ball to her teammate stationed within the penalty area. That player attempts to score by beating the two defenders on the dribble and kicking the ball past the goalkeeper. Immediately after a point is scored, the goalkeeper makes a save, or the ball goes out of play, the server plays another ball into the area and play continues. Play for 90 seconds, after which the server switches places with her teammate and the round is repeated. Play a series of 90-second rounds; teams switch roles every two rounds.

Scoring: Award 1 point for a shot on goal saved by the goalkeeper and 2 points for a goal scored. Teammates total their points to get the team score. The team scoring the most points wins.

Practice tips: Encourage defenders to double down on the attacker to prevent penetration on the dribble and shots on goal. Adjust the size of the playing area to accommodate the ages and ability of your players.

Minutes: 15

Players: Unlimited (groups of 3)

Objectives: To execute the wall (give-and-go) pass to beat a defender; to defend in an outnumbered situation

Setup: Place markers to create a 15-yard-square area for each group. Designate two players as attackers and one as defender. You'll need one ball per group.

Procedure: Attackers attempt to keep the ball from the defender by dribbling, shielding, and passing to each other. Emphasize use of the give-and-go (wall) pass to beat the defender. To perform a wall pass, the player on the ball commits (dribbles at) the defender, passes to his teammate who is positioned to the side, and immediately sprints behind the defender to collect a one-touch return pass. If the defender steals the ball, he immediately returns it to the attackers, and the game continues. Play three 5-minute rounds; each player takes a turn as the defender.

Scoring: Attackers earn 1 point for five passes without a possession loss and 2 points each time they execute a wall pass to bypass the defender. The player conceding the fewest points when playing as the defender wins the competition.

Practice tips: Successful execution of the wall pass requires skill, timing, anticipation, and teamwork. The player with the ball must commit the defender. At the same time, the supporting teammate must position himself to create an open passing lane to the ball. Increase the area size for beginning players to allow attackers more time to execute skills and make decisions.

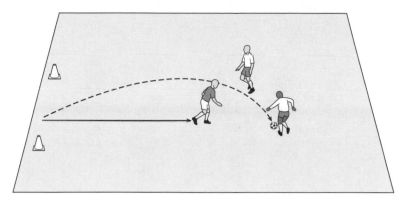

Minutes: 15

Players: 3

Objectives: To improve the ability to attack and defend in a 2v1 situation; to develop dribbling, passing, and tackling skills

Setup: Use markers to create a 15-yard by 30-yard field area. Have one player (defender) stand on an end line with a ball. The remaining two players (attackers) begin on the opposite end line facing the defender.

Procedure: The defender initiates play by serving the ball to the attackers, and then moves forward off the end line to close the distance. The attackers control the ball and advance to take on the defender 2v1. The objective is to penetrate past the defender, either via the dribble or by executing a give-and-go pass, and dribble the ball over the end line. Attackers must stay within the 15-yard-wide channel when attempting to beat the defender. The round ends when the defender steals the ball, the ball leaves the field area, or the attackers advance the ball under control over the end line, whichever occurs first. Players immediately return to their original positions and repeat the round.

Scoring: Award the defender 1 point for stealing the ball or for forcing the attackers to play the ball out of the area. Attackers score 1 point when they penetrate past the defender and dribble the ball across the end line. Play to 10 points, after which players rotate positions and repeat. Play 3 rounds; each player takes a turn as the defender.

Practice tips: Attackers should dribble at (commit) the defender at speed. The defender should attempt to delay the attackers, anticipate their actions, and act appropriately. Encourage attacking players to recognize opportunities to execute the wall pass.

Minutes: 20

Players: 4 (2 teams of 2)

Objectives: To execute the wall pass to beat an opponent; to defend in an outnumbered situation; to rehearse an immediate transition between attack and defense

Setup: Use markers to create a 15-yard-wide by 25-yard-long area for each game. Position cones or flags to represent a goal 4 yards wide at the midpoint of each end line. Organize two-player teams for competition. One team has the ball to begin. No goalkeepers required.

Procedure: Begin with a kickoff from the center of the field. Each team defends a goal and can score in the opponent's goal. The team with the ball attacks with two players; the defending team has one player as the goalkeeper and the other as a single defender. Change of possession occurs when the defender steals the ball, the goalkeeper makes a save, the ball going out of the field area was last touched by an attacker, or a point is scored. A defender who steals the ball must pass it back to her goalkeeper before the team can counterattack. After receiving the ball, either from a teammate or by making a save, the goalkeeper immediately moves forward to join her teammate to attack the opponent's goal. One player on the opposing team immediately sprints back to play as goalkeeper, while her teammate plays as the single defender. Teammates should alternate turns playing as the goalkeeper.

Scoring: Award 1 point for each goal scored. The team scoring the most points wins.

Practice tips: Emphasize quick transitional play on change of possession. Encourage attackers to run at and commit the defender, and then execute the wall (give-and-go) pass to penetrate past the defender.

Minutes: 15

Players: Unlimited (groups of 4)

Objectives: To provide support to teammates at the proper angle and depth; to pass and receive the ball effectively under gamelike pressures; to defend in an outnumbered situation

Setup: Use markers to create a 10-yard by 15-yard area for each group. Designate three players as attackers and one as the defender. One ball required per group.

Procedure: Attackers try to keep the ball from the defender by dribbling and passing among themselves. If the defender steals the ball or kicks it out of the area, the attacker whose error caused the loss of possession immediately becomes the defender, and the original defender joins the attack.

Scoring: The attacking team scores 1 point for eight consecutive passes without possession loss. The defender conceding the fewest points wins the competition.

Practice tips: Encourage attacking players to position themselves at the correct angle and depth of support to provide clear passing lanes for the teammate with the ball. Impose restrictions to make the game more challenging (such as limiting attackers to three touches or fewer to pass and receive the ball). For beginners, increase the playing area size and reduce the number of consecutive passes required to score.

116 Last Player in Defends ⚽⚽

Minutes: 15

Players: 5

Objectives: To develop proper angles of support among attacking players; to improve passing skills and decision-making ability under gamelike pressures

Setup: Use markers to create two 12-yard by 12-yard (square) grids spaced approximately 10 yards apart. Place three or four balls outside of each square. Designate four players as attackers and one as a defender. Three attackers and the defender begin in square 1. The remaining attacker (target) starts in square 2.

Procedure: The attackers in square 1 attempt to keep the ball from the defender. Attackers must complete at least four consecutive passes within the square before passing the ball to the player (target) in square 2. The three attackers then sprint into square 2 to support their teammate there. The last player to arrive in square 2 becomes the defender in that square; the others combine to play 3v1 against the defender. The original defender remains in square 1 as the target player for the next round.

Play is continuous as players move back and forth from one square to the other. If the defender steals the ball or kicks it out of the square, the attacker who lost possession of the ball becomes the defender, and the game continues. If the pass to the target in the opposite square is not accurate (within the square), the player who made the errant pass becomes the defender.

Scoring: Four consecutive passes within a square followed by an accurate pass to the target in the opposite square scores 1 point.

Practice tips: Emphasize proper support for the player on the ball. Attackers should generally position themselves at wide angles of support (greater than 45 degrees) to prevent the outnumbered defender from cutting off the passing lane.

Minutes: 20 (5-minute rounds)

Players: 8 (2 teams of 2 plus 4 support players)

Objective: To improve the combination play and support movement required to keep the ball from opponents

Setup: Use markers to outline a 30-yard-square playing area. Place a cone at the midpoint of each side of the square. Position a support player near each cone. Remaining players partner with a teammate to create two teams of two. Both teams begin within the playing area; one team has the ball. Use colored vests to differentiate teams.

Procedure: The team in possession attempts to keep the ball from its opponents for as many passes as possible. Support players assist the team in possession to create a 6v2 player advantage for the attack. However, support players are restricted in their movements—they can move laterally along their sideline but are not permitted to move inward off the line. Support players are also limited to two touches to receive and pass the ball. In addition, support players may receive the ball from and pass it to the central players only; they may not pass among themselves. Loss of possession occurs when a defending player steals the ball or the ball goes out of play. Play for 5 minutes, after which central players switch roles with support players. Play a total of four rounds.

Scoring: Award 1 team point for eight passes without a possession loss. The team scoring the most points wins.

Practice tips: Impose restrictions to make the game more challenging for advanced players, such as limiting support players to one touch or prohibiting them from passing the ball back to the player from whom they received the ball. Reduce the area size and award 1 point for five consecutive passes to make the game more manageable for younger players.

(118) 2v2 (+Targets) ⚽⚽

Minutes: 15

Players: 6 (2 teams of 2 field players and 1 target player each)

Objectives: To combine with a teammate to penetrate opposing defenses; to coordinate the defensive concepts of pressure and cover

Setup: Use markers to outline a 20-yard by 30-yard field. Form two teams of three players each. Each team defends an end line of the field; two players from each team position themselves to defend their end line while the remaining (target) player from each team starts on the end line opposite his teammates. One ball required per game; an extra supply of balls placed nearby is recommended.

Procedure: Teams play 2v2 within the area, each team defending an end line. Goals are scored by passing the ball to the team's target player who is on the opposing team's end line. Target players are permitted to move laterally along the end line to create clear passing lanes for their teammates. Defending players try to prevent opponents from completing a pass to the target playing on their end line. Change of possession occurs after a goal is scored, when the ball goes out of bounds off an attacking player, or when a defending player steals the ball. Play for 5 minutes, after which the target players switch positions with one of their teammates. Play three 5-minute games so that all players get an opportunity to play as the target.

Scoring: The attacking team scores 1 point for a pass completed to the target player on the end line behind the defending team. The team scoring the most points in 5 minutes wins.

Practice tips: As a variation, add sideline support players to the game to create a greater numerical advantage for the attacking team.

Minutes: 20

Players: 6 (2 teams of 3)

Objectives: To practice group tactics used in attack and defense; to coordinate movement of the first (pressuring) and second (covering) defenders; to improve transition play

Setup: Place markers to create a 20-yard by 30-yard playing area. Place two cones or flags 5 yards apart at the midpoint of each end line to represent goals. Organize two three-player teams. Use colored vests to differentiate teams. One team has the ball to begin.

Procedure: Begin play with a kickoff from the center of the field. Each team defends a goal. The team who gets possession attacks with three players; opponents defend with two field players and a goalkeeper. A defending player who steals the ball must pass it back to her goalkeeper before initiating an attack on the opponent's goal. After receiving the ball, the goalkeeper moves forward to join her teammates to form a three-player attack. One player on the opposing team immediately retreats into the goal to play goalkeeper; the remaining two players position themselves to defend the goal. Play is continuous with teams switching between attack and defense at each change of possession. Teammates take turns playing as the goalkeeper for their team.

Scoring: Goals are scored by kicking the ball through the opponent's goal below head height. The team scoring the most goals wins.

Practice tips: Emphasize immediate transitions between defense and attack on change of possession. Place extra balls behind each goal to avoid delays when a ball is shot past the goal. Adjust the area size to match the ages and abilities of your players.

(120) Split the Defense ⚽⚽

Minutes: 24

Players: Groups of 6 (4 attackers, 2 defenders)

Objectives: To practice the combination play required to penetrate an opposing defense; to coordinate the movement of the first (pressuring) and second (covering) defenders

Setup: Place markers to create a 10-yard by 20-yard area for each group of six. Designate four players as attackers and two as defenders. Use colored vests to differentiate attackers from defenders. All players stand within the playing area. One attacker has the ball to begin.

Procedure: Attackers attempt to keep the ball from the defenders. When possible, they should split (pass the ball between) the two defenders. This type of pass is commonly referred to as the *killer* pass because it penetrates the defense and puts defenders at a great disadvantage. If a defender steals the ball, or if the ball leaves the playing area, the ball is immediately returned to an attacker, and the game continues. Play for 8 minutes; then designate two different players as defenders for the next round. Play three rounds; all players take a turn as defenders.

Scoring: The attacking team scores 1 point for eight consecutive passes without a loss of possession and 2 points for a pass that splits the defenders. The defending team conceding the fewest points in 8 minutes wins.

Practice tips: Attacking players should constantly adjust their positions as the ball changes location to maintain clear passing lanes to the ball. Support players should position themselves at wide angles on either side of the ball. The defender nearest to the ball (first defender) should apply pressure on the ball to limit the time and space available to the attacker. The defender farthest from the ball (second defender) positions himself to protect the space behind the first defender and to prevent the killer pass. For highly skilled players, reduce the area size and limit the number of touches allowed to pass and receive the ball.

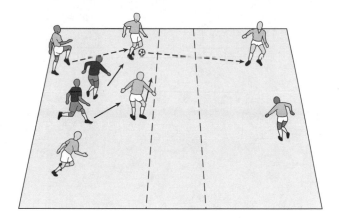

Minutes: 20

Players: 8 (6 attackers, 2 defenders)

Objectives: To possess the ball with the ultimate goal of penetrating the defense; to practice defending when in an outnumbered situation

Setup: Use markers to create a 20-yard by 35-yard area divided into two grids (1 and 2), each 15 yards by 20 yards with a 5-yard-deep neutral zone between them. Place four attackers and two defenders in grid 1 and two attackers in grid 2. Use colored vests to differentiate attackers from defenders. Attackers in grid 1 have possession of the ball to begin. No goalkeepers are required. Place a supply of balls outside of each grid.

Procedure: The four attackers in grid 1 play keep-away from the two defenders. Attackers are limited to three or fewer touches to pass and receive the ball. After completing five or more consecutive passes, the attackers in grid 1 can pass the ball to the attackers stationed in grid 2. Two of the four attackers in grid 1 immediately follow the ball into grid 2 to join the two attackers already stationed there. The two defenders also sprint into grid 2 to challenge for the ball there, creating another 4v2 situation in grid 2. If a defender steals the ball or the ball travels outside of the grid, attackers immediately put another ball into play, and the game resumes. Play for 5 continuous minutes; then designate two different defenders and repeat the activity. Play a total of four rounds so each player gets a chance to play as a defender.

Scoring: Defenders score 1 point each time they force a loss of possession. The pair scoring the most points wins the competition.

Practice tips: Emphasize quick ball movement, fast decision making, and proper angles of support for attacking players. Emphasize possession with the ultimate goal of penetration (passing to the adjacent grid), and not merely possession for possession's sake.

Minutes: 16 to 20

Players: 6 (4 attackers, 2 defenders)

Objectives: To coordinate the movement of the first (pressuring) and second (covering) defenders; to develop individual tackling skills; to improve fitness

Setup: Use markers to create a 20-yard-square playing field. Station two defenders in the center of the area; position one attacker at the midpoint of each sideline. Place a server (coach) outside the grid with an ample supply of balls.

Procedure: The server passes a ball to one of the attackers. The player receiving the ball attempts to dribble through the square to the opposite side of the square. The two defenders position themselves to deny penetration; the first defender pressures the attacker while the second provides cover. If the attacker cannot immediately penetrate into the space behind the defenders, she passes to one of the attackers stationed on an adjacent side. Upon receiving the ball, that player immediately attempts to dribble across the square to the opposite side. Defenders must immediately readjust their positions to deny penetration by the new attacker. If the ball is stolen by a defender or kicked out of the grid, the server immediately plays another ball to a different sideline attacker. An attacker who dribbles to the opposite sideline is awarded 1 point; she then returns to her original position by running along the outside of the square. Play for 4 minutes and then designate two new defenders. Each player should take a turn as a defender.

Scoring: Award 1 point to an attacker who dribbles through the grid to an opposite sideline. The attacker scoring the most points wins the game.

Practice tips: Emphasize immediate pressure on the ball by the first defender. Defenders must quickly readjust positions when the ball is played to a different attacker. Attackers stationed on the sides can move along the line to make themselves available to receive a pass from the player with the ball when that player cannot penetrate the defense via the dribble.

Minutes: 15

Players: 8 (2 teams of 4)

Objectives: To practice the combination play required to penetrate an opposing defense; to defend in an outnumbered situation

Setup: Position markers to create a 20-yard by 30-yard field for each group. Organize two teams of four players each. Place two minigoals, each 4 yards wide, at the corners of each end line. One ball required per game.

Procedure: Each team defends the two goals on its end line and can score in either of the goals on the opponent's end line. The team with possession attacks with four players; the opponents defend with two players, and their two remaining teammates drop back into the goals to play as goalkeepers. Attacking players are limited to three touches or fewer to pass, receive, and shoot the ball. If a defending player steals the ball, he must pass it back to one of the goalkeepers after which all four players attack the opponent's goals. The team that lost possession drops two players into its goals to play as goalkeepers.

Scoring: The attacking team scores 1 point for kicking the ball through either of the defending team's goals past the goalkeepers. The team scoring the most points wins the game.

Practice tips: Emphasize immediate transitions between defense and attack on change of possession. Attacking players should move the ball quickly in attempts to unbalance the outnumbered defenders and create passing and shooting lanes. Defending players must position themselves to defend the most critical space and attempt to force attackers to shoot from poor (wide) angles.

Minutes: 20

Players: 7 (2 teams of 3 plus 1 neutral player)

Objectives: To practice group attack and defense tactics; to improve passing, receiving, and dribbling skills under gamelike pressures of limited time and restricted space

Setup: Use markers to create a 35-yard-square playing area. Organize two teams of three players each. Designate one additional player as a neutral player who always joins the team with possession of the ball. Use colored vests to differentiate teams and the neutral player. You will need one ball per game. Award one team possession of the ball to begin.

Procedure: The team with the ball attempts to keep it from the opponents. The neutral player joins the team in possession to create a 4v3 player advantage for the attack. Change of possession occurs when a defending player steals the ball or when a ball going out of play was last touched by a member of the attacking team. Play is continuous with teams switching between attack and defense on each change of possession. There are no restrictions on the number of touches permitted to receive and pass the ball, so attacking players can combine dribbling and passing skills to maintain possession.

Scoring: Award 1 point for six consecutive passes without a loss of possession. The team scoring the most points wins.

Practice tips: Encourage quick ball movement along with proper positioning of support players. On defense, emphasize the concepts of pressure, cover, and balance to limit attacking options and ultimately win possession of the ball. You can reduce the time and space available to more experienced players by decreasing the area size.

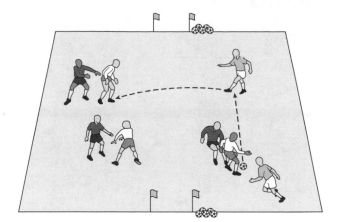

Minutes: 20

Players: 8 (2 teams of 3 plus 2 neutral players)

Objectives: To coordinate group tactics in attack and defense; to practice quick counterattack; to improve fitness

Setup: Use markers to create a field 25 yards wide by 40 yards long. Position flags to create a goal 4 yards wide at the midpoint of each end line. Organize two teams of three players each and designate two additional players as neutrals who always play with the team in possession of the ball. Use colored vests to differentiate teams and neutral players. There are no goalkeepers. You'll need one ball per game. Place an extra supply of balls in each goal.

Procedure: Award one team the ball. Begin with a kickoff from the center of the area. Neutral players join the team with the ball to create a 5v3 player advantage for the attack. Teams score by kicking the ball through the opponent's goal. Players on the team with possession are restricted to three or fewer touches to pass, receive, and shoot the ball. A defending player who wins the ball must first pass it to one of the neutral players before initiating the counterattack. Otherwise, regular soccer rules apply.

Scoring: The team scoring the most goals wins.

Practice tips: Emphasize immediate transitions between defense and attack on each change of possession. Advanced players can use regulation-sized goals and goalkeepers. Reduce the area size for younger players.

126 **Two-Sided Goals** ⚽ ⚽ ⚽

Minutes: 15 to 20

Players: 10 (2 teams of 5)

Objectives: To develop effective passing combinations and off-the-ball player movement; to practice changing the point of attack; to improve general endurance

Setup: Position markers to create a field 30 yards wide by 40 yards long. Use flags or cones to represent a goal three yards wide in each half of the field, about 10 yards in from the end lines. Organize two teams of equal numbers. Use colored vests to differentiate teams. There are no goalkeepers. You'll need one ball per game.

Procedure: Award one team possession of the ball and begin with a kickoff from the center of the area. Teams can score points through either goal; in addition, goals may be scored from either side of the two-sided goals. Each team must defend both goals when the opponents have the ball. The offside rule is waived. Otherwise, regular soccer rules apply.

Scoring: The team scoring the most goals wins.

Practice tips: Stress the importance of immediate transitions between defense and attack on change of possession. Teams should try to quickly change the point of attack (location of the ball) to attack the goal least defended. Add restrictions if desired (such as a limited number of touches). You can also add a neutral player to the game who always joins the team in possession.

Minutes: 25

Players: 10 (3 teams of 3 plus 1 neutral goalkeeper)

Objectives: To practice the group tactics used in attack and defense; to improve fitness; to provide goalkeeper training

Setup: Play on one end of a regulation field with a full-sized goal centered on the end line. Use markers to extend the penalty box to 36 yards from the goal, creating a field area 36 yards long and 44 yards wide. Organize three teams of three players each. The first team sets up to defend the goal, and the second team begins, with the ball, on the end line facing the goal. Players from the third team spread themselves on the perimeter of the playing area. The goalkeeper stands within the goal.

Procedure: The team with the ball enters the field to attack the goal; the opponents defend. Players from the third team serve as neutral passing outlets for the team with possession; they cannot enter the field but can move laterally in support of the ball. The team in possession can pass to the neutral players, who must return the ball into the field with two touches or fewer. Change of possession occurs when the ball goes out of the area, a goal is scored, the goalkeeper makes a save, or a defender steals the ball. After a save, the keeper tosses the ball toward a corner, and both teams compete for possession. Play is continuous, with the two competing teams alternating between attack and defense with each change of possession. The goalkeeper is neutral and attempts to save all shots.

Scoring: The team scoring a goal stays in the field for the next round; the team conceding a goal becomes the neutral team. The team scoring the most goals at the end of time wins the game.

Practice tips: Virtually all group tactical concepts can be demonstrated in a 3v3 situation. Emphasize the attacking concepts of width, depth, and penetration. Emphasize the defensive principles of pressure (first defender), cover (second defender), and balance (third defender).

Minutes: 25

Players: 12 (3 teams of 3 plus 1 neutral player and 2 goalkeepers)

Objectives: To rehearse group attack and defense tactics; to improve endurance

Setup: Organize three teams (A, B, C) of three players each. Designate an additional player as a neutral who always joins the team in possession. Use markers to create a 40-yard by 75-yard field with a regulation goal on each end line. Divide the field into three 40-yard-wide by 25-yard-long zones. Begin with team A in the middle zone with the ball. Teams B and C are positioned in opposite end zones to defend the goals. Place a goalkeeper in each goal. The neutral player joins the team in possession (team A) in the middle zone. Use colored vests to differentiate teams.

Procedure: Team A, assisted by the neutral player, moves forward out of the middle zone to attack one of the goals. The defending team gains possession of the ball when it intercepts a pass, when the goalkeeper makes a save, when a goal is scored, or when a ball traveling over the end line was last touched by the attacking team. On change of possession, the original defending team sprints into the middle zone, where it is joined by the neutral player and attacks the opposite goal. The team that lost possession (team A) remains in the end zone to defend during the next round of play. The neutral player always joins the team with the ball to produce a 4v3 player advantage for the attack. Play is continuous as teams attack one goal and then the other.

Scoring: The team scoring the most goals wins.

Practice tips: Encourage players to perform at game pace. The team gaining possession should sprint into the middle zone, quickly organize, and then attack at speed. In actual match situations, any delay in the attack allows additional defenders time to recover to offset the numerical advantage.

Minutes: 20

Players: 8 (2 teams of 4)

Objectives: To rehearse the concepts applying to zonal defense

Setup: Use markers to create a 20-yard-long by 35-yard-wide field area. Place additional markers to divide the area lengthwise into three zones. The end zones (1 and 3) are 10 yards wide by 20 yards long; the middle zone (2) is 15 yards wide by 20 yards long. Place cones or flags to represent a small goal (2 to 3 yards wide) on opposite end lines of each zone (six total). You'll need one ball per game. Have an additional supply of balls available. Use colored vests to differentiate teams.

Procedure: Organize two teams of four. Each team is responsible for defending the three goals on its end line and may score in the opponent's three goals. One player from each team stands in zones 1 and 3. These players defend the team's goal in these zones. Two players from each team play in zone 2 and are responsible for defending the goal in that zone. Defending players are restricted to moving within their zone. There are no restrictions on the team with the ball; attacking players can move between zones to overload a zone if they want. However, if there is a change of possession, they must immediately return to their assigned zone. Otherwise, regular soccer rules apply.

Scoring: Award 1 point for each goal scored.

Practice tips: As a variation, allow one player in the middle zone to slide sideways into an end zone to provide support (defensive cover) for the teammate in that zone. Similarly, allow defending players in the end zones to slide laterally into the middle zone to provide cover and balance for the central defenders. Emphasize proper defensive shape and balance. Zonal positioning is based on the location of the ball and the position of defending teammates.

Minutes: 25

Players: 12 (2 teams of 4 plus 2 neutral wingers and 2 goalkeepers

Objectives: To emphasize effective flank play; to improve the ability to score off crossed balls; to defend serves into the goal area

Setup: Play on a 40-yard-wide by 60-yard-long field area, with a full-sized goal centered on each end line. Position markers to form a 5-yard-wide channel on each flank, extending the length of the field. Organize two teams of four players, using colored vests to differentiate teams. Designate two additional players as neutral wingers, one in each flank channel. Place a goalkeeper in each goal. One ball is required per game, with an extra supply of balls placed behind each goal.

Procedure: Teams compete 4v4 in the middle channel of the field. Each team defends a goal and can score in the opponent's goal. The neutral wingers, who are restricted to movement within their flank channel, join the team with possession to create a 6v4 player advantage for the attacking team. Goals can be scored directly from shots originating in the middle channel or from balls crossed into the goal area by the wingers. When a winger receives the ball from a central player or the goalkeeper, he must dribble forward at speed toward the opponent's end line and cross the ball into the goal area. Otherwise, regular soccer rules apply.

Scoring: Award 1 point for each goal scored from a shot originating within the middle channel, and 2 points for a goal scored directly off a crossed ball. The team scoring the most points wins.

Practice tips: This game reinforces the use of flank play to open up an opponent's defense. It also provides training for the goalkeeper in handling crossed balls.

Minutes: 20

Players: 12 (2 teams of 5 players plus 2 neutral players)

Objectives: To practice group attack and defense; to practice a sudden shift in the point of attack to exploit open space

Setup: Play on a 30-yard-wide by 40-yard-long field area. Use markers to represent three 3-yard-wide goals on each end line. One goal is at each corner and the third goal is at the center of the end line.

Procedure: Organize two teams of five players each. Designate two additional players as neutrals who always join with the team in possession to create a 7v5 player advantage for the attacking team. Each team defends the three goals on its end line and can score in the three goals on the opponent's end line. Players on the team in possession are restricted to three or fewer touches to receive, pass, and shoot the ball. Play is continuous, with an immediate transition between defense and attack on each change of possession.

Scoring: Passing the ball through a goal counts as 1 point. The team scoring the most points wins the game.

Practice tips: Encourage attacking players to move the ball quickly in order to unbalance defenders and create gaps of space within the defense. The defending team members must stay compact, adjust their positions as a group to maintain proper defensive shape, and position themselves to control the most dangerous attacking space.

CHAPTER 8

Large-Group and Team Tactical Games

Soccer tactics are applied at three levels—individual, small-group, and large-group or team. Individual tactics encompass the principles of attack and defense that apply in one-on-one situations. Small-group tactics involve three or more players in combination. Tactics are also applied to the team as a whole, particularly regarding player roles and systems of play. The ultimate objective of large-group or team tactics (7v5, 9v6, and so on) is to make the whole team greater than the sum of its individual parts.

At this point, players should understand the responsibilities of the first, second, and third defenders and the role they play in team defense, as well as the role of first, second (supporting), and third attackers. The next step in the team-building process is to incorporate these strategies into an overall plan for team attack and defense. My years of experience as a player and coach have made me aware that a group of talented individuals does not necessarily form a cohesive team. Effective team play requires that teammates work together in an organized and disciplined manner. Players must be physically fit, they must play with commitment and determination, and above all, they must fulfill their specific roles in team attack and defense. Large-group tactical games can foster such development by placing players in situations where they must choose the best course of action (such as whether to pass or dribble, tackle or delay) from a multitude of options.

Team tactics channel the collective efforts of the 11 individuals constituting a soccer team toward a common goal. Players can improve their ability to combine with teammates by developing a clear understanding of what the team is trying to accomplish when the opponents have the ball as well as what the team is trying to do when they have possession. The games described in this chapter can serve greatly in that regard.

It is important to realize that at its most fundamental level, the game of soccer is not about formations. Soccer is about players—their strengths, their weaknesses, their personalities, their character—as individuals working in concert with others to create a whole that is greater than the sum of its parts. There are no magical formations that will transform ordinary players into great players or suddenly change a weak team into a dominant team. So although the system of play provides structure and defines a starting point for team tactics, it should never be the primary focus. The technical and tactical concepts reinforced in the large-group tactical games described in this chapter are universal to all systems of play. Although individual player roles and responsibilities may differ from one formation to another, the principles of attack and defense associated with these games apply to all systems, and in that way they enhance player development.

Successful team play is predicated in large part on the decisions players make in response to changing situations during play. Poor decisions will eventually translate into goals scored against the team; good decisions ultimately lead to individual and team success. The following games require players to make split-second decisions under gamelike conditions, which in turn will improve their decision-making skills on the soccer field.

Minutes: 20

Players: 14

Objectives: To maintain possession through the use of dribbling skills coupled with passing combinations; to practice defending as a group

Setup: Use markers to designate a 20-yard by 30-yard field. Organize a team of six defenders and a team of four attackers; designate four additional players as neutral players who always join the defending team when it has possession of the ball. Attackers and defenders play within the area; the neutral players are located along the perimeter of the field area, one on each sideline. A server (coach) stands outside of the field area with a supply of balls. The six-player defending team has the ball to begin.

Procedure: The defending team tries to keep the ball from the attacking team. Defenders are limited to three or fewer touches to receive and pass the ball and can pass to the neutral players as well as to their teammates. Neutral players are permitted to move laterally along the sidelines and are restricted to two touches to receive and pass the ball. Neutral players can only return the ball to a defender within the field. When an attacker steals the ball, the attacking team attempts to keep possession. Because attackers are outnumbered, they do not have a touch restriction; they can use whatever means necessary (passing, dribbling, shielding, and so on) to keep the ball from the defenders. However, attackers *may not* use the neutral players as passing options. If the ball goes out of the field area, the server immediately sends another ball into play. Neutral players switch roles with attackers every five minutes or so.

Scoring: The defending team scores 1 point for six or more consecutive passes without a loss of possession. Attackers score 1 point for possessing the ball for 30 seconds or more at a stretch.

Practice tips: Emphasize pressure, cover, and balance in defense; focus on individual ball possession skills on attack.

Minutes: 25

Players: 13 (7 attackers and 5 defenders plus 1 goalkeeper)

Objective: To practice the group tactics used in attack and defense

Setup: Play on half of a regulation field with a full-size goal centered on the end line. Position markers to represent two 3-yard-wide minigoals placed 20 yards apart on the halfway line. Designate a team of seven to play against a team of five and a goalkeeper. Use colored vests to differentiate teams. The goalkeeper plays in the regulation goal; there are no goalkeepers in the minigoals. You'll need one ball per game. An extra supply of balls is recommended.

Procedure: Organize the seven-player team as two strikers, four midfielders, and an anchor player behind the midfielders. Organize the five-player team as four defenders and a holding midfielder fronting the defense. The seven-player team attempts to score in the regulation goal and defends the minigoals. The five-player team gains possession of the ball by intercepting passes, tackling the ball away from an opponent, or receiving the ball from the goalkeeper after a save has been made. The five-player team can score through either of the small goals on the halfway line. Play is continuous.

Scoring: The seven-player team scores 2 points for a goal and 1 point for a shot on goal saved by the goalkeeper. The five-player team scores 1 point by kicking the ball through either of the small goals. The team scoring the most points wins.

Practice tips: The five-player team, since it is outnumbered, must be positioned to protect the most central areas from which goals are most likely to be scored. Impose restrictions to make the game more challenging for the seven-player team (such as two- or three-touch passing only) or to emphasize specific aspects of attacking and defending tactics.

Minutes: 25

Players: 12 to 16

Objectives: To coordinate team attack and defense; to improve player ability to compete in 1v1 situations; to develop individual dribbling, shielding, and tackling skills

Setup: Position markers to create a 50-yard-wide by 70-yard-long field. Organize two equal-size teams; use colored vests to differentiate them. Position one team in each half of the field. You'll need one ball per game.

Procedure: Begin with a kickoff from the center of the field. Regular soccer rules are in effect except for the method of scoring. Goals are scored by dribbling the ball across the opponent's end line rather than by shooting. The entire length of the end line is considered the goal line. There are no goalkeepers.

Scoring: Teams score 1 point for dribbling the ball under control across the opponent's end line. The team scoring the most points wins.

Practice tips: Require one-on-one defensive marking, with each player assigned a specific opponent. The fundamental principles of team attack and team defense apply. Players should take on (attempt to dribble past) opponents only in certain situations and areas of the field. Encourage players to take on opponents in the attacking third of the field, the area nearest the opponent's end line. Beating an opponent on the dribble in that area will create a scoring opportunity, so the risk of possession loss is more than compensated for by the potential benefit. Discourage players from taking on opponents by dribbling in the team's defending third (the part of the field nearest their end line), where possession loss might lead to a goal against the team.

Minutes: 20

Players: 12 to 16 (2 equal-size teams of 5 to 8 plus 2 goalkeepers)

Objectives: To encourage appropriate use of dribbling skills in game situations; to develop endurance

Setup: Position markers to create a 40-yard-wide by 60-yard-long field with a regulation goal centered on each end line. Divide the field into three 20- by 40-yard zones. Organize two teams of equal numbers. Place a goalkeeper in each goal. Use colored vests to differentiate teams. One ball is required per game; an extra supply of balls is recommended.

Procedure: Begin with a kickoff from the center of the field. Each team defends a goal and can score in the opponent's goal. Regular soccer rules are in effect except for the following: (1) Players may use three touches or fewer to pass and receive the ball when in the defending third of the field nearest their goal; (2) in the middle zone, players are permitted to dribble to advance the ball when they are in open space, but they are not allowed to take on and beat opponents on the dribble; and (3) in the attacking third of the field, players must beat at least one opponent on the dribble before passing to a teammate or shooting on goal. Violating the zone restrictions results in a loss of possession to the opposing team.

Scoring: The team scoring the most goals wins.

Practice tips: Dribbling skills are used most effectively in the attacking third of the field, an area where the risk of possession loss is outweighed by the possibility of creating a goal-scoring opportunity. Players should be encouraged to take on opponents in the attacking third. Excessive dribbling, particularly in the defending and middle thirds of the field, should be discouraged because these are areas where loss of possession often translates into scoring opportunities for the opponent.

Minutes: 25

Players: 22 (2 teams of 8 plus 4 goalkeepers and 2 neutral players)

Objectives: To constantly change the point of attack to relieve defensive pressure; to develop effective counterattack combinations; to improve physical endurance

Setup: Position markers to create a 60-yard-wide by 75-yard-long field. Place two full-size goals on each end line, spaced about 25 yards apart. Have one team in each half of the field with a goalkeeper in each goal. Use colored vests to differentiate teams. One team has the ball to begin.

Procedure: Each team defends the two goals on its end line and can score in the opponent's two goals. Neutral players join the team with possession to create a 10v8 player advantage for the attack. Otherwise, regular soccer rules are in effect.

Scoring: The team scoring the most goals wins.

Practice tips: Encourage players to attack the most vulnerable (least defended) goal. They can do so by quickly switching the point of attack to unbalance defenders and expose opponent's weaknesses. To make the game more challenging, impose restrictions on advanced players (such as limiting players to two touches to pass and receive the ball).

Minutes: 25

Players: 19 (10-player team and 7-player team plus 2 goalkeepers)

Objectives: To develop effective transition play in attack and defense; to rehearse group and team attack and defense tactics

Setup: Play on a regulation field with a full-size goal on each end line. Place a line of markers the width of the field, approximately 35 yards from each end line, to divide the field into three zones. Organize a team of ten and a team of seven; use colored vests to differentiate teams. Place a goalkeeper in each goal. You'll need at least one ball; an extra supply of balls is recommended.

Procedure: Begin with a kickoff from center field. Each team defends a goal and may score in the opponent's goal. The 10-player team must use three or fewer touches to pass and receive the ball; otherwise, regular soccer rules are in effect. The 7-player team has no touch restriction. The coach or an assistant coach should serve as referee. Every few minutes, whistle a halt in play and award the 7-player team a direct free kick from their defending zone. When the kick is taken, all members of the 10-player (defending) team must be in the middle zone. The 7-player team must serve a long pass off the free kick into the space behind the 10-player (defending) team. Opposing players are not permitted to enter their defending zone, marked by a 35-yard line, until a player from the 7-player team enters the zone and touches the ball. At that point, players can immediately track back in an attempt to defend their goal.

Scoring: Award 1 point for a shot on goal saved by the goalkeeper and 2 points for a goal scored. The team scoring the most points wins.

Practice tips: Encourage teammates to move forward quickly as an organized unit when on the attack. Defending players should play as a compact unit and must make swift and direct recovery runs to protect the space behind the defense.

Minutes: 20 to 25

Players: 20 (3 teams of 6 plus 2 goalkeepers)

Objective: To use the width and depth of the field to attack an outnumbered defending side

Setup: Use markers to create a 40-yard-wide by 60-yard-long field with a full-size goal centered on each end line. Organize three teams of six players each. Teams A and B begin within the field area; each team defends a goal. Players from team C are positioned along the perimeter of the field as neutrals, one on each sideline and two along each end line. Use colored vests to differentiate teams. Put a goalkeeper in each goal.

Procedure: Teams A and B compete against one another. Players can use the sideline and end line neutral players (team C) as passing options when in possession of the ball, creating a 12v6 player advantage for the attack. Neutral players may not enter the field area, but they can move along the perimeter lines. Sideline neutrals are allowed two touches to receive and pass the ball; end line neutrals must return the ball into the field using only one touch. Play for 5 minutes or until a goal is scored (whichever comes first), after which players from one of the middle teams (A or B) switch places with team C, and the game continues. Play several rounds.

Scoring: Award 1 point for a goal scored. The team scoring the most goals wins.

Practice tips: The attacking team should use the neutral players to create scoring opportunities. Players should vary the type and distance of their passes, including long passes behind the opposing defense to the neutral players stationed on the end lines. Impose restrictions (two-touch, three-touch, and so on), depending on the age and ability of players.

Minutes: 20 to 25

Players: 18 (2 teams of 8 plus 2 goalkeepers)

Objectives: To develop total team support when advancing from the defending into the attacking thirds of the field; to coordinate group passing combinations

Setup: Play on a 65-yard-wide by 75-yard-long field divided into three 65- by 25-yard zones. Position a full-size goal at each end of the field. Form two teams (team A and team B) of eight players each. Each team begins with three players in its defending third, three players in the middle third, and two players in the attacking zone (3-3-2 alignment). Use colored vests to differentiate teams. Have a goalkeeper in each goal. Award one goalkeeper the ball to begin.

Procedure: To begin play, the goalkeeper distributes the ball to a teammate within the team's defensive third of the area. Players can advance the ball to the middle zone by dribbling or by completing a pass to a teammate, after which one player originally stationed in the defensive third moves to the middle zone, creating a 4v3 player advantage in that zone. The four teammates in the middle zone try to combine to pass or dribble the ball into the attacking third. If successful, one teammate from the middle third moves to the final third to create a 3v3 player situation. Players from the defending team may not cross zones; they must defend in their assigned zones only. Teams reverse roles on each change of possession or after a goal is scored. Otherwise, regular soccer rules are in effect.

Scoring: Award 1 point for a goal scored. The team scoring the most points wins.

Practice tips: Teams should practice "safety first" in their defending third, where possession loss can prove costly. Players can take greater risks in the attacking third, where loss of possession is not as critical. Impose restrictions to emphasize specific concepts or to make the activity more difficult. For example, limit players to two touches in their defending third, three touches in the middle third, and unlimited touches in the attacking third.

Minutes: 25

Players: 20 (2 teams of 9 field players plus 2 goalkeepers)

Objectives: To exploit the open space behind the opponent's defense; to practice a direct style of attack, from back to front, employing accurate passes over distance

Setup: Play on a regulation field with a full-size goal centered on each end line. Use markers or lines to designate an offside line 30 yards from each end line. Have teams begin on opposite halves of the field, between the offside lines. One goalkeeper is in each goal. Use colored vests to differentiate teams. One ball is required; an extra supply in each goal is suggested.

Procedure: Begin with a kickoff from the center spot. Regular soccer rules apply, except for a variation of the offside rule. A player from the attacking team can be as far forward as the offside line, located 30 yards from the opponent's goal, and not be considered offside even if she is behind the last defender. This rule variation prevents the defending team from compressing the field and enables the attacking team to play long passes into the open space behind the last line of defending players.

Scoring: Regular scoring is in effect; the team scoring the most goals wins the game.

Practice tips: Encourage teams to take advantage of the liberal offside rule. When possible, back players should look to play the ball into their deep-lying targets. As a variation, limit players to two touches in their own half of the field. This encourages quick ball movement and more direct play.

Minutes: 20

Players: 20 (2 teams of 10)

Objectives: To use combination passing and ball movement to keep the ball from an opposing team; to practice the defensive principles of immediate pressure and cover

Setup: Use markers to outline a 50-yard-square field area, bisected by a midline. Organize two teams of 10 players each; differentiate teams with colored scrimmage vests. Begin with one team in each half of the field. One ball is required; have a supply of extra balls placed around the field area.

Procedure: Award one team possession of the ball to begin. That team attempts to keep the ball from its opponents within its half of the field. Five players from the opposing team enter that half of the field to win the ball, creating a 10v5 situation in that area. Players on the team with possession are permitted two touches to receive and pass the ball. When the defending team wins the ball, players must pass it to a teammate in the opposite half of the field and then sprint to join the team. The team losing possession immediately sends five players into the opposite half of the field to regain possession. Play continues back and forth between halves with each change of possession. The ratio of attackers to defenders is always 10v5 in each half.

Scoring: None; teams should strive to possess the ball as long as possible in their half.

Practice tips: Encourage players to receive and pass the ball quickly and efficiently and to change the point of attack (location of the ball) often. The key to success is to play a simple game and to use supporting teammates as passing options. The defending team, outnumbered 10 to 5, must pressure the ball and limit passing options in order to gain possession.

Minutes: 15

Players: 16 (2 teams of 8)

Objectives: To practice attacking and defending as a group, utilizing the principles of team attack and defense

Setup: Position markers to outline a 30-yard-wide by 40-yard-long field area, with a 5-yard deep end zone at each end of the field. Organize two teams of eight players each; differentiate teams with colored scrimmage vests. Each team defends an end zone. Four players from each team start within the field area to defend their end zone; the remaining four team members are positioned in their respective end zones, spaced evenly apart. One ball is required per game; an extra supply of balls is recommended.

Procedure: Award one team possession of the ball. The four players within the field area attack the opponent's end zone, while their four teammates rest in the team's own end zone. The four defending players try to prevent the attacking team from passing or dribbling the ball into their end zone. All passes must be on the ground; chipping balls over the defending team is not permitted. If the attacking team passes a ball to an opponent stationed in the defending team's end zone, it counts as a score. Immediately after a score or loss of possession, the two groups of players within the field area switch places with their teammates in the end zones, and the game continues.

Scoring: Award 1 point for dribbling or passing the ball into the opponent's end zone. The team scoring the most points wins the game.

Practice tips: The defending team must employ immediate pressure on the ball and be positioned to deny penetrating passes that split the defense. Conversely, the attacking team should employ quick ball movement to unbalance the defending side to create gaps within the defense.

(143) 10v5 Breakout ⚽⚽⚽

Minutes: 15

Players: 15 (plus a server/coach)

Objectives: To maintain possession of the ball against a greater number of opposing players; to initiate an immediate breakout (counterattack) upon gaining possession of the ball

Setup: Position markers to outline a 30-yard-wide by 40-yard-long grid. Organize three teams of five players each. Teams wear different-colored vests. All players start within the grid. The coach (or server) stands outside of the grid with a supply of six to eight balls. Designate one team as the defenders for the first round, the other two as attackers.

Procedure: Two teams of five attackers join forces to keep the ball from the defending team, creating a 10v5 player advantage. The server initiates play by passing a ball into the field area to one of the attacking players. Attackers are limited to three or fewer touches to receive and pass the ball. If a defending player wins the ball, he attempts to play (pass) the ball to a defending teammate who is breaking out of the grid. Defending players are permitted to break out over any of the four sidelines. The attacking team tries to prevent the breakout. After a breakout, or if the ball leaves the playing area inadvertently, the server plays another ball into the attacking team and the game continues. Play until the supply of balls is depleted. Repeat the game with a different team defending.

Scoring: Award the attacking teams 1 point for eight or more consecutive passes without loss of possession. Award the defending team 1 point for each breakout. The team scoring the most points wins the round.

Practice tips: Attacking players should use the width and depth of the field area to spread the defenders and create open passing lanes. Conversely, the defending team must apply pressure in the area of the ball to limit passing options in order to disrupt the attack and force errors.

Minutes: 20

Players: 22 (2 teams of 10 field players plus 2 goalkeepers)

Objectives: To develop the attacking combinations required to create goal-scoring opportunities; to defend in an outnumbered situation

Setup: Play on an 80-yard-long by 50-yard-wide field area bisected by a mid-line. Place a regulation goal on each end line. Organize two teams of 10 players each, plus goalkeepers. Each team positions 6 players in the opponent's half of the field, and 4 players in their own half, creating a 6v4 situation in each half. Goalkeepers are in their respective goals. One ball is required; an extra supply of balls in each goal is recommended.

Procedure: The coach begins play by serving a ball into one of the six-player attacking groups who try to score on the four defenders and goalkeeper in their half of the field. If a defender wins the ball, she must pass it to a teammate in the opposite half of the field to initiate an attack on the opponent's goal. The team losing possession attempts to prevent passes into their own half. Play is continuous for 20 minutes. Regular soccer rules are in effect.

Scoring: The team scoring the most goals wins the game.

Practice tips: The group of six attacking players should utilize the width and depth of the field to unbalance the four defenders and create scoring opportunities. Conversely, the outnumbered defenders should attempt to limit attacking options, apply pressure at the point of attack, and keep the play (ball) in front of them.

Minutes: 20

Players: 18

Objectives: To improve the team's ability to keep the ball away from opponents under the pressure of limited space and time; to change the point of attack in response to defensive pressure

Setup: Play between the penalty areas of a regulation field. Position three 5-yard-wide goals along the top edge of each penalty area, 12 yards apart. Organize two teams of nine players each. Teams begin in opposite halves of the field, and defend the three minigoals on their end line. Teams can score in any of the opponent's three goals. No goalkeepers required. One ball is in play.

Procedure: Teams play 9v9 on the six minigoals. Regular soccer rules are in effect, other than there are no corner kicks and the offside law is waived—everything out of play is returned with a throw-in from the touch line.

Scoring: A ball kicked through a minigoal below waist height counts as 1 point. The team scoring the most points wins the game.

Practice tips: To make the game more difficult, you can restrict players to three or fewer touches to receive and pass the ball, or reduce the field area to further restrict the time and space available to pass and receive the ball.

Minutes: 20

Players: 18 (16 field players plus 2 goalkeepers)

Objectives: To practice attacking combinations with service from wide areas; to defend crosses into the goal area

Setup: Play on a 50-yard-long by 25-yard-wide field area, divided by a midline. Position a regulation goal on each end line. Organize two teams of eight players each, plus goalkeepers. Teams are differentiated by colored scrimmage vests. Goalkeepers are in opposite goals.

Procedure: Four players from each team start within the field area. The remaining players from each team are positioned along the perimeter lines of the offensive half of the field (the half of the field their team is attacking), two on each touchline. Perimeter players may combine with their teammates within the field area, but they may not enter the field area, nor are they permitted to pass the ball to one another. The perimeter players are limited to two touches to receive and pass the ball. They are encouraged to drive crosses into the goal area when possible. The defending team (the team without possession) defends with four players only; their perimeter players are inactive until their team gains possession and advances into the opponent's half of the field. Every few minutes the inside and perimeter players switch roles. Play is continuous for 20 minutes.

Scoring: The team scoring the most goals wins the game.

Practice tips: Encourage players to use their wide support teammates to alleviate pressure and stretch the opposing team. Perimeter players should serve crosses into the goal area, when possible, to create gamelike scoring opportunities.

Minutes: 20

Players: 20 (2 teams of 8 field players and 4 goalkeepers)

Objectives: To practice a direct style of play by serving long-driven balls into deep targets; to provide goalkeepers with practice receiving high balls

Setup: Play on a regulation field. Divide the group into two teams of eight field players and two goalkeepers each. Place markers to outline a 15- by 15-yard square in each corner of the field. Teams are located in opposite halves of the field to begin; the goalkeepers are positioned in one of the two corner squares near their end line. One ball is required; an extra supply of balls near each corner square is recommended.

Procedure: Begin with a kickoff from the center of the field. Points are scored by serving the ball into one of the opposing team's corner squares so that the goalkeeper can receive the ball directly out of the air. Otherwise, regular soccer rules are in effect. Players are encouraged to serve balls into the opposing goalkeepers at every opportunity and, when possible, from distance. To deny service into their goalkeepers, the defending team must apply immediate pressure in the area of the ball. When a goalkeeper receives the ball, he immediately distributes it to a teammate and play continues. Field players are not permitted to enter the corner squares.

Scoring: Award 1 point for a ball served into an opposing goalkeeper that is received directly out of the air. The team scoring the most points wins the game.

Practice tips: Encourage attacking players to move the ball quickly into areas where they can serve a long ball into a goalkeeper. The defending team must react accordingly to deny space and time in which to prepare and serve the ball.

Minutes: 20

Players: 20 (2 teams of 9 players plus 2 additional neutral players)

Objectives: To maintain possession of the ball; to create opportunities to play the ball forward to a deep-lying target player

Setup: Play on a 50-yard-wide by 80-yard-long field. Organize two teams of 9 players (8 players are within the field area and 1 player, the target player, stands behind the opponent's end line). Designate 2 additional players as neutral players who always join the team in possession of the ball to create a 10v8 advantage for the attacking team. No goalkeepers required.

Procedure: Regular soccer rules are in effect other than the method of scoring. The ultimate objective is for the team to complete a pass to its target player who is stationed behind the opponent's end line. The target player may move laterally along the end line to show for a pass but may not enter the field area. The defending team tries to cut off passing lanes and prevent passes into the target player. When a defending player steals the ball, that team immediately goes on the attack and is joined by the neutral players. When a player completes a pass to the team's target player, she switches places with the target; the original target then joins her teammates on the field.

Scoring: A pass completed to the target player counts as 1 point. The team scoring the most points wins the game.

Practice tips: In order to maintain possession of the ball, players must provide teammates early support at the proper angles. Players should pass the ball quickly and change the point of attack frequently in order to unbalance opponents and create passing lanes to the target player.

(149) Hold the Lead ⚽⚽⚽

Minutes: 20 (2 10-minute minigames)

Players: 20 (1 team of 8, one team of 10, and 2 goalkeepers)

Objectives: To protect a one-goal lead with a few minutes remaining in the game.

Setup: Play on a 50-yard-wide by 75 yard-long-field, with a regulation goal on each end line. Organize a team of 10 field players and a team of 8 field players. Have a goalkeeper in each goal. One ball is required; a supply of extra balls in each goal is recommended.

Procedure: Teams begin in opposite halves of the field and defend the goal on their end line. The 8-player team begins the game with a 1-0 lead. The 10-player team gets possession of the ball to begin; the 8-player team attempts to protect the 1-goal lead by utilizing the defending principles of immediate pressure on the ball, cover and balance behind the ball, and defensive compactness. Regular soccer rules are in effect. The game is 10 minutes in duration. If the 10-player team or the 8-player team scores before 10 minutes have expired, that team wins the match, and the game ends. Repeat the game with teams switching roles; take two players from the 10-player team and add them to the 8-player team.

Scoring: A goal scored by either team ends the minigame and results in a win for the team that scored. If neither team scores before time expires, the 8-player team wins the minigame.

Practice tips: Defending players must be organized to deny open space and time to the attacking team. The defensive principles of pressure at the point of attack, cover, and defensive balance away from the ball should be emphasized. The 10-player attacking team should work on changing the point of attack, playing quickly and directly, and serving the ball into the danger zone front and center of the goal when possible.

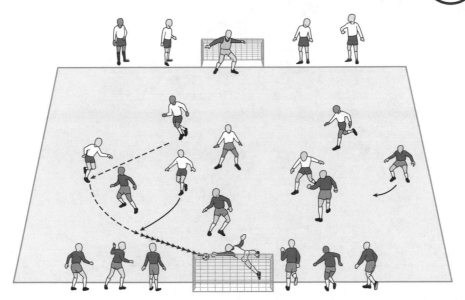

Minutes: 20 (series of 2-minute rounds)

Players: 22 (2 teams of 10 plus 2 goalkeepers)

Objectives: To practice attacking at speed when in a numbers-up situation; to defend in a numbers-down situation

Setup: Play on a shortened (40-yard-long and 50-yard-wide) field with a goal centered on each end line. Organize two teams of 10 players and a goalkeeper. Each team designates 6 of its players as attackers and 4 as defenders. Teams line up on their respective end lines with the goalkeeper in goal. The coach (server) stands on a sideline, near the midline, with a large supply of balls.

Procedure: To begin the coach kicks a ball toward one of the end lines. The team there receives the ball and attacks the opponent's goal with the six players designated as attackers; their opponents defend with the four players designated as defenders. The attacking team has 120 seconds in which to score a goal. After each shot or ball out of play, the coach immediately serves another ball into the attacking team and play continues. After a goal is scored, or 120 seconds have elapsed, whichever comes first, the teams return to their respective end lines to organize for round two. The coach then serves a ball to the original defending team, who then attacks with their six designated attackers. Repeat for a predetermined number of two-minute rounds.

Scoring: A goal scored ends the round. Team scoring the most goals wins.

Practice tips: Attacking players in a numbers-up situation should attack with speed, use direct play, and serve balls into the dangerous scoring zone front and center of the goal when possible. The defending team must protect the most dangerous scoring zones by positioning players goal side of the ball and eliminating the most dangerous attacking space.

Minutes: 20

Players: 16 (2 teams of 7 field players and a goalkeeper)

Objectives: To practice scoring from outside the penalty area; to provide forwards with opportunities to score off rebounds; to provide goalkeeper training

Setup: Play on a 40-yard-long by 30-yard wide field area divided by a midline. Place a regulation goal at the center of each end line. Organize two teams of seven field players and a goalkeeper. Each team begins with five players (midfielders) in its defending half of the field and two players (strikers) in the opponent's half to create a 5v2 situation in each half. Place a supply of balls in each goal.

Procedure: Award one team the ball to begin. To initiate play, the goalkeeper distributes the ball to a teammate in the defending half of the field. The five teammates in that zone move the ball quickly to create an opportunity to shoot on the opponent's goal. All shots must originate from within the team's defending half (20 yards or more from the opponent's goal). The two strikers stationed in the attacking half of the field can finish rebounds off the goal or the goalkeeper, but they are not permitted to receive passes directly from teammates stationed in the opposite half. The two strikers can create their own scoring opportunities if they can steal the ball from opponents within their designated half of the field. Players must remain in their assigned zones throughout the game.

Scoring: The team scoring the most goals wins the game.

Practice tips: The emphasis is on long-range shooting by midfielders and follow-up shots by the strikers. Strikers can get their share of "garbage goals" just by being in the right place at the right time, so they should become accustomed to following up every shot on the opponent's goal.

Minutes: 20

Players: 20 (2 teams of 8 plus 4 neutral players)

Objectives: To respond to defensive pressure by quickly passing the ball into areas least defended by opponents in order to create scoring opportunities

Setup: Play within a 50-yard-square field area. Use cones or discs to represent a triangular goal with 5-yard-long sides in each of the four corners of the field, about 10 yards into the field from the corner. Organize two teams of eight players each. Designate four additional players as neutral players who always play with the team in possession. Assign each team two goals to defend, and two goals to attack. Award one team possession of the ball to begin.

Procedure: All players are limited to three or fewer touches to receive and pass the ball. The team with possession is joined by the neutral players to create a 12v8 player advantage for the attack. Change of possession occurs if the defending team steals the ball, if the ball that goes out of play was last touched by the attacking team, or if an attacking player uses more than three touches to receive and play the ball. Goals are scored by kicking the ball through any side of the three-sided triangular goals. Change of possession does not occur after a goal is scored; the team scoring retains possession.

Scoring: Award 1 point for a ball kicked through any side of a triangular goal. The team scoring the most points wins the game.

Practice tips: Emphasize quick ball movement, limited touch, and frequent changing of the point of attack.

Minutes: 20-25

Players: 18

Objectives: To practice the defensive principles of pressure, cover, balance, and compactness within a competitive game situation

Setup: Play on a 90-yard-long by 60-yard-wide field. Use two lines of small discs to divide the field into three 20-yard-wide vertical zones extending the length of the field. Place two minigoals (3 yards in width) on each end line, at the points where the end lines intersect with the disc lines. Organize two teams of nine players each. Both teams align in a 3-4-2 formation. No goalkeepers are required.

Procedure: Award one team the kickoff at the center of the field. Each team defends the two goals on its end line and can score in the opponent's goals. Regular soccer rules are in effect. The emphasis in this game is on defensive compactness, so the defending team should attempt to compact the space on the side of the field where the attacking team is trying to score. To do so, all players on the defending team should slide toward that side of the field so that all defenders are in the same vertical third, or the adjacent third, of the field when a shot is taken on goal. The overall emphasis is on reducing the space available to attacking players.

Scoring: A goal scored is worth 1 point. If a defending player is located in the far zone (farthest from the goal) at the moment goal is scored, then the attacking team is awarded 2 additional points.

Practice tips: The defending team must utilize all of the fundamental principles of team defense to deny penetration and win the ball. Conversely, the attacking team should attempt to stretch the defense by quick ball movement coupled with constant changing of the point of attack.

Minutes: 20

Players: 18 (2 teams of 7 field players and 2 goalkeepers plus 2 neutral players)

Objectives: To push players forward into the attack when in possession of the ball; to defend in an outnumbered situation

Setup: Play on a 70-yard-long by 50-yard-wide field area with a full-size goal centered on each end line. Place a small goal (5 yards wide) on each side of the full goal, close to the corners of the field. Use markers to divide the field into three zones 25 yards deep at each end and 20 yards deep in the middle. Organize two teams of seven field players and a goalkeeper; designate two additional players as neutral players who join the team in possession of the ball, to create a 9v7 player advantage for the attacking team. Position a goalkeeper in each full-size goal. One ball is required; place a supply of extra balls in each goal.

Procedure: Teams defend the three goals on their end line and can score in any of the opponent's three goals, although scores in the full-size goal count double. Other than the method of scoring, regular soccer rules are in effect. In addition, a team cannot score until all of its players are pushed forward into the attacking and middle zones—no player is permitted to be in the team's defending zone when the shot is taken. In such a case, the goal does not count.

Scoring: A score in the full-size goal is worth 2 points; a score in a smaller flank goal is worth 1 point. The team scoring the most points wins the competition.

Practice tips: Encourage the attacking players to use the width and depth of the field to stretch the defense and create gaps of space in which to penetrate with the ball.

CHAPTER 9

Goalkeeping Games

The goalkeeper is the only player on the team permitted the use of hands to receive and control the ball. Additionally, keepers must perform a unique set of skills that differ in many respects from those used by the field players. Top-flight keepers combine a high degree of mental toughness with outstanding physical ability. Goalkeepers must be proficient at receiving shots arriving on the ground and through the air. They must be able to catch and hold powerful shots that arrive from different angles and distances and must be willing to propel their bodies through the air to make the save or dive at the feet of an onrushing opponent to smother the ball on a breakaway. Goalkeepers must develop a thorough mastery of angle play in order to be positioned to the best advantage. In short, the goalkeeper must be willing do whatever it takes to make the big save—and preventing goals is only half the job! Once the save has been made, the keeper is responsible for initiating the team's attack by distributing the ball accurately to teammates.

Physical challenges aside, from a psychological standpoint, the goalkeeper also occupies the most demanding position on the field. Although each member of the team must accept responsibility for any physical and mental errors committed during the heat of competition, mistakes by the keeper are generally punished more immediately and more severely. Simply put, a mistake by the goalkeeper in most instances results in a goal against the team. It is not a position for the faint of heart or weak of spirit. To consistently perform at a high level, the goalkeeper must couple outstanding physical tools with a high degree of mental toughness.

That being the case, I find it somewhat surprising that the keeper is typically the player most neglected during training sessions. She often spends the bulk of practice standing in the goal with explicit orders to stop all shots. Obviously that is not sufficient training for the team's last line of defense, the final barrier preventing an opponent's score. The soccer goalkeeper is a specialist, much like goalkeepers in hockey and lacrosse, and must be trained as such. The practice games described in this part are most appropriate for intermediate and advanced players who have previously been introduced to basic goalkeeper skills. The games can be used to sharpen those skills as well as to supplement more intense goalkeeper training.

It is generally accepted that players under 12 years old should not specialize solely in the goalkeeper position. Most are not physically mature enough to perform some of the requisite drills, such as diving to save or distributing the ball via the javelin toss over great distances. It is also important for all young players, including those who think that they ultimately want to be a goalkeeper, to develop the fundamental foot skills commonly used by field players. These include various types of short- and long-range passes as well as the ability to receive and control passes from their teammates (rules prohibit the keeper from using the hands to control a ball that is passed back to her from a teammate). The constantly changing role of the goalkeeper requires that she be able to perform foot skills much more so than in the past.

Minutes: 10

Players: Unlimited (in pairs)

Objective: To improve a goalkeeper's ability to catch and hold the ball; to develop *soft* hands

Setup: Pair goalkeepers for the exercise. Partners stand approximately four yards apart, facing one another. Each holds a ball in the right hand at about head height.

Procedure: Partners simultaneously toss a ball from their right hand to their partner's left hand while shuffling sideways across the width of the field. Tosses are received on the fingertips with one hand only. Return the ball by tossing it with the left hand to the partner's right hand. Partners continue shuffling back and forth across the width of the field 10 times.

Scoring: Assess 1 penalty point each time a goalkeeper drops the ball or makes an inaccurate toss. Each player keeps track of her own penalty points. The keeper accumulating the fewest number of points wins.

Practice tips: Maintain balance and body control at all times. Players should not cross their legs when shuffling sideways. Make the game more challenging by increasing the velocity of tosses.

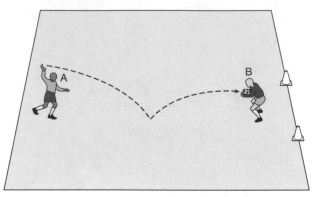

Minutes: 15

Players: Unlimited (in pairs)

Objective: To save low-driven shots using the forward vault technique

Setup: Pair goalkeepers (A and B) for competition. Use markers to outline a 15-yard-wide by 20-yard-long field area for each pair. Position flags to represent a 5-yard-wide goal on each end line. Goalkeepers stand in opposite goals. Goalkeeper A has the ball to begin.

Procedure: Goalkeeper A throws or half-volleys the ball so that it bounces (skips) off the ground directly in front of B, who attempts a save using the forward vault technique (described under Practice tips). If keeper B fails to hold the ball, keeper A may follow up the shot and score off the rebound. After each save or goal, keepers return to their respective goals and repeat in the opposite direction. Play for a specified time or predetermined number of shots.

Scoring: Award 1 point for a ball held without rebound. The goalkeeper who scores the most points wins.

Practice tips: The keeper must develop the ability to save and hold low-skipping shots, particularly when field conditions are wet and slippery. To do so the keeper should align himself with the oncoming ball and dive forward to smother the shot, clutching the ball between forearms and chest. Elbows and arms should be cradled underneath the ball to prevent it from bouncing free. Goalkeepers should not try to catch the low-skipping shot directly in their hands, because this increases the risk of a rebound.

Minutes: 10

Players: Unlimited (in pairs)

Objective: To improve a goalkeeper's ability to catch and hold powerful short-range shots

Setup: Partners face one another at a distance of about 10 yards. One ball is required for this exercise; having a few extra balls nearby is recommended.

Procedure: Keepers *ping*, or volley, the ball back and forth to one another. All volley kicks should be directed at the partner's chest or head so that diving to save is not necessary. Keepers attempt to catch and hold the volley and then return the ball to their partner in a similar manner.

Scoring: Award 1 point for each volley that is caught and held without a rebound. The keeper who scores the most points wins.

Practice tips: Encourage goalkeepers to position themselves behind the ball as it arrives, with arms extended forward and slightly flexed at the elbow. Palms should face forward with fingers spread and slightly extended. The ball is received on the fingertips and palms, with hands extended and the head behind the ball. Keepers should withdraw their hands slightly on contact with the ball to cushion the impact.

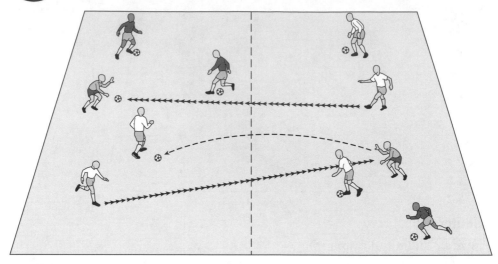

Minutes: 10 to 15

Players: 10

Objective: To improve the goalkeeper's ability to receive low- and medium-height balls

Setup: Position markers to outline a 40-yard-wide by 60-yard-long field area, divided by a midline. One goalkeeper and four field players start in each half of the field. Each field player has a ball.

Procedure: Field players in both halves of the field dribble randomly with a ball. Every few seconds, the goalkeepers simultaneously shout out the name of a player dribbling in the opposite half of the field. That player quickly drives a low shot at the goalkeeper in the opposite half of the field. The keeper receives the ball using the appropriate technique, returns the ball by throwing to the player who kicked it, and then calls out the name of a different player. Continue the exercise for several minutes as keepers receive low- and medium-height balls.

Scoring: Goalkeepers are penalized 1 point if they fail to hold the shot. The goalkeeper conceding the fewest penalty points wins the game.

Practice tips: Encourage goalkeepers to square up with the shooter and move forward to meet the ball as it arrives. Field players can vary the service between ground balls and knee-high shots.

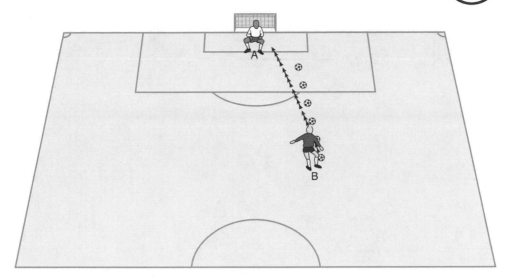

Minutes: 15

Players: 2 goalkeepers

Objectives: To practice saving shots originating from different spots within the penalty area; to develop mobility and footwork

Setup: Play on one end of a regulation field. One goalkeeper (A) starts in the goal; the other goalkeeper (B) places a line of six balls that lead toward the goal. The first ball is placed about 15 yards from the end line, in line with one of the goal posts. The other balls are lined up with the first, at distances of 12, 10, 8, 6, and 4 yards out from the goal post.

Procedure: Goalkeeper B (shooter) takes six shots in succession, beginning with the ball farthest from the goal and continuing down the line of balls. Goalkeeper A attempts to save all shots. To do so, after each save attempt keeper A must quickly reposition and set in order to save the next shot, which will be coming from a slightly different shooting angle. After six shots, the goalkeepers switch positions and repeat the round. Play a total of 8 to 10 rounds.

Scoring: Goalkeepers are awarded 1 point for each save, for a possible 6 points per round. The goalkeeper totaling the most points wins the match.

Practice tips: The defending goalkeeper should try to hold each shot, or at least parry the shot wide of the goal. After each shot, the defending keeper should reposition and set, according to the location of the ball, to narrow the shooting angle.

160 Reaction Saves ⚽⚽

Minutes: 15 to 20 minutes

Players: 4 goalkeepers

Objectives: To save close-range volley shots

Setup: Play on one end of a regulation field with a full-sized goal. Position markers to form a 4-yard square 12 yards front and center of the goal. Organize two teams of two goalkeepers each (A and B; C and D). Goalkeeper A begins in the goal and her teammate B stands to one side of the goal; Goalkeeper C stands in the center of the 4-yard square and her teammate D stands on the other side of the goal.

Procedure: To begin, goalkeeper B kicks a low-driven ball to Goalkeeper C. C receives the ball using a *scoop save* with forearms cradled underneath the ball, and then tries to score on A by volleying the ball out of the hands into the goal. After the shot, A and B switch positions, as do C and D. Repeat for 10 volleys on goal, and then have teams switch locations and repeat. Play a total of five rounds (50 shots on goal) for each team.

Scoring: The team conceding the fewest goals wins the competition.

Practice tips: Goalkeepers get practice receiving ground balls with the scoop technique as well as making sudden reaction saves on the powerful close-in volley shots. As a variation, you can position a lone forward 5 to 7 yards in front of the goal to finish any balls that the goalkeeper does not hold.

Minutes: 20

Players: 6 (4 shooters and 2 goalkeepers)

Objective: To improve shot-saving ability; fitness training

Setup: Pair goalkeepers for competition. Play on one end of a regulation field with a full-sized goal. Place 16 balls an equal distance apart on the front edge of the penalty area (18 yards from goal). Station four shooters about 25 yards from goal. One of the goalkeepers stands in the goal.

Procedure: Shooters alternate attempting to score from a one-time strike of a stationary ball. After each save or score, the next shooter immediately initiates her approach to a ball. Allow the keeper just enough time to set in the ready position in preparation for the next shot. Continue the exercise until the supply of balls is depleted; then reposition balls for the next round with a different goalkeeper. Play a total of six rounds, three for each goalkeeper.

Scoring: Award the goalkeeper 1 point for each save. The keeper scoring the most points wins the match.

Practice tips: The goalkeeper should wear appropriate clothing (padded shorts, long-sleeved shirts with padded elbows) to reduce the incidence of bumps and bruises from repeated diving to save. Reduce the shooting distance for younger players.

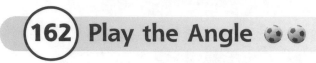
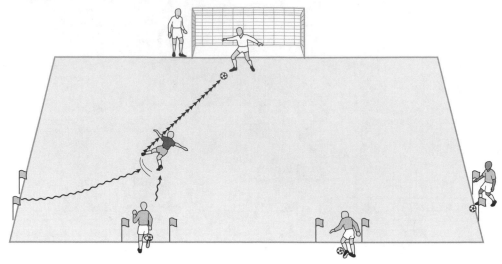

Minutes: 15

Players: 6 (4 shooters and 2 goalkeepers)

Objectives: To improve angle play; to provide shot-saving practice

Setup: Play on one end of a regulation field. Use markers to represent four gates, each three yards wide—one gate near each corner of the front edge of the penalty area and one on each side of the penalty area. Place a shooter behind each gate, each with a supply of three balls. The goalkeeper starts in the goal.

Procedure: Shooters, in turn, dribble through their respective gates and shoot on goal from a distance of 12 yards or greater. The goalkeeper can advance off the line to narrow the shooting angle and make the save. After each shot or save, the goalkeeper returns to the goal, sets in the ready position, and prepares to save the next shot. Each shooter takes 3 shots, for a total of 12 shots for the round. Repeat with a different goalkeeper in goal.

Scoring: The goalkeeper scores 1 point for each save. The goalkeeper totaling the most points wins the competition. Play at least four rounds.

Practice tips: Focus on proper footwork and optimal positioning to reduce the shooting angle. The keeper should set his feet just prior to the shot.

Minutes: 15

Players: 6 (4 servers and 2 goalkeepers)

Objective: To improve throwing accuracy

Setup: Play on half of a regulation field with a regulation goal on the end line. Use markers to represent five 3-yard-wide goals at various locations within the field—one goal within the center circle, one on each flank area about 35 yards from the end line, and one at each front corner of the penalty area. One goalkeeper starts in the regulation goal, and the other rests to the side of the goal. Station the servers at various spots outside of the penalty area, each with a supply of balls.

Procedure: Servers, in turn, drive balls into the goal area. After receiving the ball, the keeper immediately distributes to imaginary teammates by throwing the ball through one of the minigoals. Continue the exercise until the keeper has attempted 3 tosses at each minigoal for a total of 15 throws. Repeat the round with a different goalkeeper in goal. Play 2 rounds for each keeper.

Scoring: Award 1 point for a ball tossed or rolled through either of the goals located at the edge of the penalty area, 2 points for a ball tossed through the flank goals, and 3 points for a ball that travels through the goal located in the center circle. The goalkeeper scoring the most points wins.

Practice tips: Goalkeepers can choose from several throwing techniques. The rolling (bowling) or sidearm technique can be used over short distances, whereas the baseball throw or javelin throw should be used to distribute the ball over medium and long distances. This game is not appropriate for young players who do not possess the physical strength and ability to throw the ball over distance.

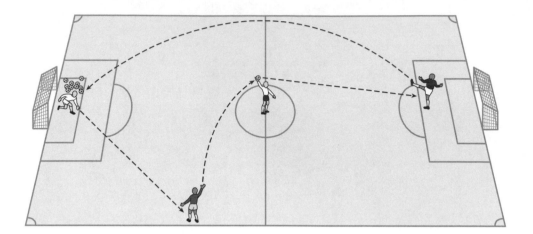

Minutes: 20

Players: 4 goalkeepers

Objective: To improve goalkeeper ability to distribute the ball accurately over various distances

Setup: Play on a regulation field with a full-sized goal on the end line. Goalkeeper A begins in the goal; B stands near a touchline, about 35 yards from goal; C begins within the center circle; and D is at the front edge of the opposite penalty area. Goalkeeper A has an ample supply of balls to begin.

Procedure: Begin the exercise with goalkeeper A distributing a ball to B, either by the rolling or sidearm-throw technique. Keeper B receives the ball and sends it to keeper C using the baseball-throw technique. Keeper C receives the ball and distributes to keeper D via the javelin throw. Keeper D returns the ball to keeper A by dropkicking or punting it the length of the field. Repeat the circuit five times, after which goalkeepers rotate positions and repeat. Play until each keeper has taken a turn at each station.

Scoring: Award 1 point for an accurate throw and 2 points for an accurate punt or dropkick. By definition, *an accurate throw* is one that does not require the intended target to move more than four steps in any direction to receive the ball. An accurate punt or drop kick is a ball driven through the air past the midline of the field that rolls into the opposite penalty area. The goalkeeper scoring the most points wins.

Practice tips: Accuracy is more important than distance when throwing or tossing the ball, at least in most situations. Distance becomes more of a priority when drop-kicking or punting. This exercise is appropriate for physically mature, experienced goalkeepers of high school age and older.

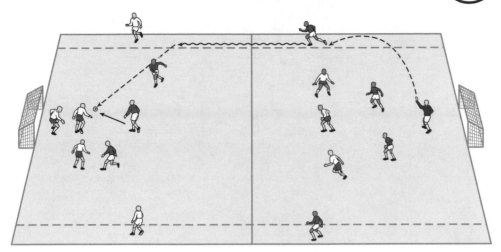

Minutes: 20

Players: 16 (4 flank players, 6 attackers, 4 defenders, and 2 goalkeepers)

Objectives: To develop the goalkeeper's ability to receive and control balls served into the goal area; to coordinate the play of the goalkeeper and defending teammates; to distribute the ball accurately by throwing

Setup: Play on a 70-yard-wide by 80-yard-long field area divided by a midline. Position a regulation goal on each end line. Place a line of markers a few yards in from each sideline to create a channel for unopposed flank players. Organize two teams of seven field players and a goalkeeper. Use colored vests to differentiate teams. Each team stands one player within each flank channel, three players (attackers) in the opponent's half of the field, and two players (defenders) in its own half. The goalkeepers start in their respective goals, each with a supply of balls. One goalkeeper (A) has the ball to begin.

Procedure: Keeper A tosses the ball to the teammate stationed in either flank channel. That player immediately dribbles unopposed the length of the channel and serves the ball into the opponent's goal area. The three teammates in that half of the field attempt to finish the cross, while the two opponents in that same half attempt to clear the ball out of the goal area. Once goalkeeper B secures the ball, or after a goal is scored, she distributes the ball to a teammate in one of the flank channels of the field, and the game continues toward the opposite goal. A crossed ball not secured by the goalkeeper is considered a live ball and can be finished by the attacking team. Play continues for 20 minutes.

Scoring: The team (goalkeeper) who concedes the fewest goals wins the game.

Practice tips: To make the game more challenging for the goalkeeper, allow flank players to dribble inward from their wide channel once they receive the ball to create a live 4v2 situation to goal. This variation will require additional adjustments for the goalkeeper.

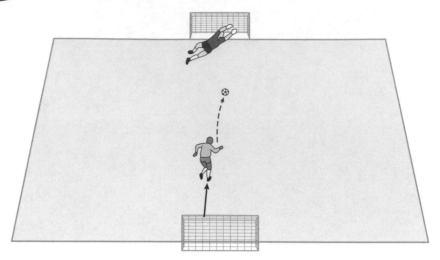

Minutes: 20

Players: Pairs

Objective: To improve shot-saving ability in a competitive setting

Setup: Pair goalkeepers (A and B) for competition. Play on a 20-yard-wide by 30-yard-long field with a full-sized portable goal on each end line; if goals aren't available, use flags to represent regulation-width goals. Keepers begin in opposite goals. Keeper A has the ball to begin. Place extra balls in each goal.

Procedure: Keeper A takes five steps forward off the goal line and attempts to volley or throw the ball past B. After a save or a goal scored, keeper B tries to score against A in the same manner. Keepers return to their goal line after each shot on goal.

Scoring: Award points for preventing goals: 2 points for a ball caught and held and 1 point for a save made by deflecting (parrying) the ball wide or over the goal. The keeper who scores the most points wins.

Practice tips: Goalkeepers should move forward off the goal line to narrow the shooter's angle. Avoid rebounds if at all possible. If keepers are not confident of holding the ball, they should deflect it out of play.

Minutes: 20

Players: 16 (2 teams of 7 field players and 2 goalkeepers)

Objective: To practice shot-saving skills in a gamelike environment

Setup: Use markers to outline a 40-yard-wide by 60-yard-long field divided by a midline. Position a full-sized goal on each end line. Organize two teams of seven and use colored scrimmage vests to differentiate teams. Each team places five players in the opponent's half of the field and two players in its own defending half, creating a five-attacker versus two-defender situation in each half. Station a goalkeeper in each goal. You'll need one ball per game; place extra balls in each goal. Award one team the ball to begin.

Procedure: One goalkeeper initiates play by distributing the ball to a teammate in the opponent's half of the field. Attacking players are permitted only two touches of the ball before they must pass to a teammate or shoot at goal. If a defender wins the ball, or the goalkeeper makes a save, he immediately plays the ball to a teammate stationed in the opponent's half of the field. Play for 20 minutes, with five attackers versus two defenders in each half. Other than the touch restriction, regular soccer rules apply.

Scoring: The goalkeeper conceding the fewest goals wins.

Practice tips: This game should produce many and varied scoring opportunities. Goalkeepers must communicate effectively with their defenders and position themselves to the best advantage to narrow the shooter's angle and make the save.

Minutes: 20

Players: 10 (2 teams of 4 field players and 2 goalkeepers)

Objectives: To improve shot-saving ability, angle play, mobility, and footwork

Setup: Play on a 50-yard-square field area. Use flags or markers to outline a 2-yard by 8-yard rectangle to represent a two-sided goal at the center of the field. Organize two teams of four field players each. Use colored vests to differentiate teams. Station a goalkeeper on each side of the two-sided goal. One keeper has the ball to begin.

Procedure: To begin, the goalkeeper tosses the ball to a far corner of the area, where both teams vie for possession. The offside law is waived and goals can be scored through either side of the goal; otherwise, regular soccer rules apply. Goalkeepers are neutral and attempt to save all shots. After each save or goal, play is restarted with the goalkeeper tossing the ball to a corner of the area.

Scoring: A shot traveling through the goal below the height of the goalkeeper's head counts as a goal scored. The goalkeeper conceding the fewest goals wins the competition.

Practice tips: Keepers will be required to make all types of saves in this game (breakaways, reaction saves, diving saves, and so on). For younger goalkeepers, designate a 5-yard-deep zone on each side of the goal where attacking players may not enter. This will help to prevent collisions between field players and the goalkeeper.

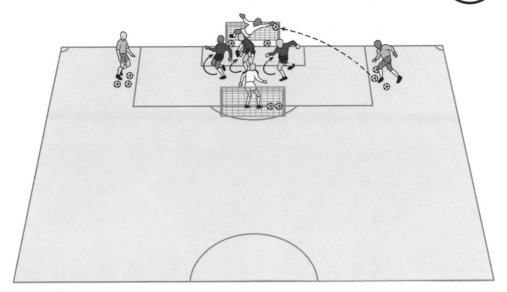

Minutes: 20

Players: 7 (1 team of 3 field players, 2 servers, 2 goalkeepers)

Objectives: To develop the goalkeeper's ability to receive and control high balls served into the goal area

Setup: Play within the 18-yard-deep and 44-yard-wide penalty area of the field. Position one full-sized goal on the end line of the field and a second goal at the front edge of the penalty area, facing the goal on the end line. Organize a team of three field players who start in the area between the two goals. Have a server on each flank, wide of the penalty area. A goalkeeper stands in each goal, each with a supply of several balls placed within the goal.

Procedure: The game begins with one goalkeeper tossing a ball to one of the wide servers who dribbles toward the opposite goal and crosses a ball into the goal area. The three-player team attempts to score all crossed balls. There are no defenders other than the goalkeeper. When a goalkeeper receives a ball served into the goal area or makes a save, she immediately distributes the ball to the server stationed on the opposite flank; this player dribbles toward the opposite goal and serves a ball into the goal area. The three-player team sprints toward that goal and attempts to score off the serve. The exercise continues, alternating from one goal to the other, until the supply of balls is depleted. Any ball that the keeper does not hold is considered to be a live ball, to be finished by the three-player team.

Scoring: The keeper conceding the fewest goals wins the game.

Practice tips: This exercise requires keepers to extend their range and coverage of the goal area. Keepers should be aggressive but not reckless in their efforts to get to the ball. They must decide which crosses they can get to and which are out of their range, and which crosses to catch and which to box away from the goal area. As a variation, add one defender at each goal, who contests the attackers for the crosses.

Minutes: 20

Players: 18 (2 teams of 4 field players plus 8 servers and 2 goalkeepers)

Objective: To provide the goalkeeper practice in handling a variety of high balls

Setup: Organize two teams of four. Use colored vests to differentiate teams. Place markers to form a playing area 40 yards wide by 50 yards long, divided by a midline. Position a full-sized goal on each end line. Each team defends a goal. Each team places two players in its defensive half of the field and two in the opponent's half. Two servers stand outside each sideline, one on each half of the field. Two more servers stand behind each end line, one to each side of the goal. Each server has several balls at his disposal. Goalkeepers begin in opposite goals.

Procedure: Number the servers one through eight and establish a sequence (order) in which they will serve balls. Play begins with the first server driving a high ball into the goal area. Teams play 2v2 in each half. Defending players try to clear the ball out of their goal area, while attacking players attempt to head or volley the ball past the keeper. The goalkeeper should attempt to play all high balls, either by catching the ball, boxing the ball, or palming it over the bar out of danger. Once a ball is cleared away or secured by the goalkeeper, or a goal is scored, the next serve is taken. Sideline servers aim their serves into the nearest goal area. End line servers lob their serves into the far goal area. Continue for 8 consecutive serves into the same goal area, then repeat the exercise to the opposite goal area. Play a total of five rounds (40 serves) to each goalkeeper.

Scoring: The goalkeeper conceding the fewest goals wins the competition.

Practice tips: Keepers should attempt to control as much of the goal area as they can, yet they should not take reckless chances that might cost their team a goal. Each goalkeeper must determine his limits and play within them.

Minutes: 20

Players: Unlimited (in pairs)

Objective: To save in a breakaway situation

Setup: Goalkeepers (A and B) pair off for competition. Use markers to outline a 20-yard-wide by 25-yard-long field. Place flags or discs to represent a goal 8 yards wide on each end line. Goalkeepers stand in opposite goals. Keeper A has the ball to begin.

Procedure: Goalkeepers alternate trying to score on one another by dribbling forward and passing the ball underneath or past their opponent, simulating a breakaway situation. Shooting is prohibited. Rebounds off the goalkeeper are playable. After each save or goal scored, goalkeepers return to their goals and repeat. Play for a specified time limit or predetermined number of scoring attempts.

Scoring: Award 1 point for each save of a breakaway situation. The keeper who scores the most points wins.

Practice tips: The defending keeper should move forward off the goal line to narrow the shooting angle and present a barrier to the attacker. Proper technique is essential. As the keeper advances, she begins to break down into a semicrouch posture with knees bent and arms extended down to sides. The keeper goes down to the side (not head first) with arms extended toward the ball to make the save.

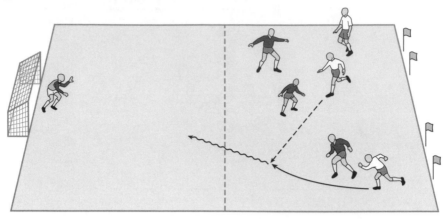

Minutes: 20

Players: 7 (2 teams of 3 plus 1 goalkeeper)

Objective: To provide goalkeeper training in breakaway situations

Setup: Use markers to form a 25-yard-wide by 40-yard-long field area, bisected by a midline. Position a full-sized goal on one end line; use flags to represent two small goals on the opposite end line. Organize two teams (A and B) of three field players each. Use colored vests to differentiate teams. You'll need one ball; a supply of extra balls is recommended.

Procedure: Station the goalkeeper in the full-sized goal. Teams A and B play 3v3 in the half of the field opposite the goalkeeper. Team A defends the full-sized goal and can score by kicking the ball through either of the two small goals on the end line on that half of the field; team B scores by dribbling the ball over the midline, which also serves as the breakaway line, and shooting into the full-sized goal. When a player from team B dribbles across the break-away line, she continues to advance unopposed at the goalkeeper, creating a breakaway situation. After the attempt on goal, regardless of whether the shot results in a goal scored or a save, the player immediately returns to the opposite half of the field, where play resumes. Play two 10-minute halves. Teams reverse roles in second half, with team A attacking the breakaway line and team B the small goals.

Scoring: Assess 2 penalty points for a breakaway goal scored against the goalkeeper. The team conceding the fewest points wins the match.

Practice tips: To avoid injury, the goalkeeper should use the proper technique when attempting to smother the ball. As she advances off the goal line toward the dribbler, the keeper begins to break down into a semicrouch posture with knees bent and arms extended down to the sides. When nearing the drib-bler, the keeper goes down on her side (not head first) with arms extended to pin the ball and make the save. As a variation, allow one defending player to chase after the attacker once she crosses the breakaway line.

Minutes: 15

Players: 12 to 16 (2 teams of 5 to 7 field players and 1 goalkeeper)

Objectives: To practice making the save in a 1v1 situation

Setup: Use markers to extend the penalty area of a field to a 36-yard-long by 44-yard-wide field area, divided lengthwise by a midline. Position a full-sized goal on each end line. Organize two teams of equal numbers, each with a goalkeeper. A goalkeeper stands in each goal; the keeper's teammates line up on the right side of their goal, each with a ball, and facing their opponents on the opposite end line.

Procedure: The first player from each team simultaneously attacks (dribbles at) the opponent's goalkeeper. Once the dribbler crosses the midline of the field, he has the option to shoot on goal or continue forward to beat the goalkeeper on a breakaway. Immediately after each score or save, the next player in line attacks the goal. Continue the game until each field player has attempted to score on the opponent's goalkeeper. Reorganize and repeat for several rounds.

Scoring: The goalkeeper conceding the fewest goals wins the match.

Practice tips: The goalkeeper can narrow the shooting angle by moving forward off the goal line as the dribbler enters the penalty area. The keeper must choose the appropriate save technique depending on the actions of the attacker.

(174) Four-Sided Goal ⚽ ⚽ ⚽

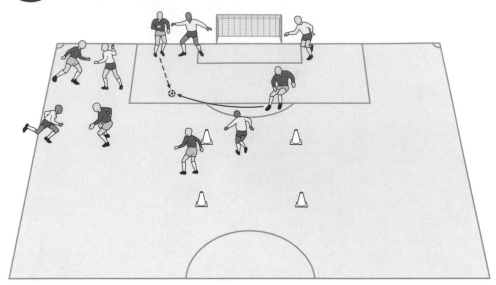

Minutes: 20

Players: 10 (2 teams of 4 field players and 1 goalkeeper)

Objectives: To develop shot-saving ability; to improve mobility and footwork; to improve angle play

Setup: Organize two teams of four field players and a goalkeeper. Use colored vests to differentiate teams. Play within half of a regulation field. Place four cones in the center of the area to form an 8-yard by 8-yard square. Each side of the square represents a goal. You'll need one ball per game; an extra supply of balls is recommended. Award one team the ball to begin.

Procedure: Begin with a throw-in from outside the playing area. Each team defends two adjacent sides of the square and can score through the other two sides of the square. Shots can be taken from any distance and any angle. The goalkeeper must defend the team's two goals—to do so, she must shuffle from one to the other depending on the movement of the ball. The offside rule is waived; otherwise, regular soccer rules apply.

Scoring: The goalkeeper allowing the fewest goals wins.

Practice tips: Goalkeepers use the side-shuffle foot movement when moving laterally into position for a save and when moving from one goal to another. Keepers should not cross their legs when moving laterally.

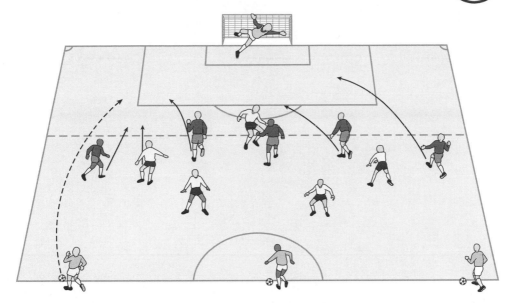

Minutes: 20

Players: 14 (2 teams of 5 fielders plus 1 goalkeeper and 3 servers)

Objectives: To practice goalkeeper communication and coordination with the defense

Setup: Play on half of a regulation field. Organize two teams of five field players each; the defending team consists of four defenders and a holding midfielder. The attacking team consists of three forwards and two midfielders. Place markers to represent a restraining line 30 yards from goal. The defending team is positioned to defend the goal. The attacking team aligns to attack the goal. Neither team can begin within the restraining line and must be at least 30 yards from goal to begin. Have three servers, each with a supply of balls, an equal distance apart approximately 60 yards from goal.

Procedure: Play begins with a server driving a ball into the open space behind the defense, beyond the restraining line. Once the ball travels past the restraining line, both teams can enter the area and compete for possession. The goalkeeper must communicate with her teammates, indicating whether she will collect the ball (shouting, "Keeper"), whether she wants the defense to clear it away (shouting, "Away"), or whether she wants the ball played back (shouting, "Back") to her. Play continues until the keeper has secured the ball, a goal is scored, or the ball has been cleared out past the 30-yard restraining line. After each round, teams are repositioned outside the restraining line and repeat the drill with a different server initiating play.

Scoring: None

Practice tips: The keeper is in a good position to see the field and direct the back line. Commands should be clear and concise, without hesitation. It is essential that the goalkeeper work in concert with her last line of defense to control the vital open space behind the defenders.

About the Author

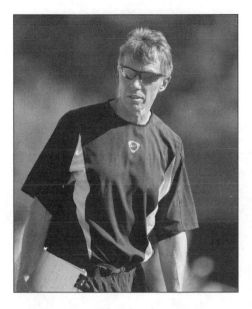

Joe Luxbacher has more than 30 years of experience in the field of competitive athletics. A former professional soccer player for the North American Soccer League, American Soccer League, and Major Indoor Soccer League, he is currently at the helm of the University of Pittsburgh men's soccer team, a position he has held since 1984.

The twice-selected Big East Conference Soccer Coach of the Year holds a PhD in health, physical, and recreation education from the University of Pittsburgh and has earned the Level A coaching license from the United States Soccer Federation.

Luxbacher has authored more than a dozen books and numerous articles on the sport of soccer. His soccer articles have appeared in national publications such as *Scholastic Coach and Athletic Director* and *Soccer Journal*.

Inducted into the Western Pennsylvania Sports Hall of Fame in 2005 and designated a Letterman of Distinction by the University of Pittsburgh in 2003, Luxbacher is the founder and director of Shoot to Score Soccer Academy, an organization that offers educational camps, clinics, and tournaments to players aged 7 to 18. The camp Web site is www.shoot2score.net.

Luxbacher resides in Pittsburgh, Pennsylvania, with his wife, Gail, and children, Eliza and Travis.